THE ART AND MAGIC OF PALMISTRY

A GUIDE TO LEARNING TO READ THE HAND

Learn to Easily Recognize
Mental, Emotional, Spiritual and Financial Inclinations

by

KOOCH DANIELS, M.A.

*Dedicated to the gods, goddesses and guides
of oracular arts and all kindred spirits who are fascinated
by the markings on hands.*

author
Kooch N. Daniels
CYBERMYSTIC.COM

design
Mark Murphy : Murphy Design Inc.
MURPHYDESIGN.COM

isbn
ISBN 978-1456342791
$20.00

COPYRIGHT ©2011 KOOCH DANIELS AND LUCKY4YOU PRESS. ALL RIGHTS RESERVED. NO PART OF THIS BOOK MAY BE REPRODUCED, STORED, OR TRANSMITTED BY ANY MEANS—WHETHER AUDITORY, GRAPHIC, MECHANICAL, OR ELECTRONIC—WITHOUT WRITTEN PERMISSION OF AUTHOR. PLEASE CONTACT KOOCH DANIELS AT U2RPSYCHIC@YAHOO.COM FOR PRESS AND ADDITIONAL INFORMATION. PLEASE RESPECT THE LAWS OF COPYRIGHT, ANY UNAUTHORIZED REPRODUCTION OF ANY PART OF THIS WORK IS ILLEGAL AND PUNISHABLE BY LAW.

BENEFITS

THIS BOOK HAS BEEN CREATED TO HELP SIMPLIFY THE ART OF PALMISTRY AND INCLUDES THE FOLLOWING BENEFITS:

{1}
Describes the most important elements of palmistry.

{2}
Simplifies learning with a speedy keyword start guide.

{3}
Gives popular topic features of essential hand analysis.

{4}
Offers uncomplicated tips to help you build skills.

{5}
Makes available a journal for recording your progress.

{6}
Provides thought provoking questions to help you learn.

{7}
Helps you look at your own hands as a palm reader.

{8}
Discusses astrology's link with palmistry.

{9}
Offers a demonstration reading.

{10}
Gives you a timeless palmistry reference.

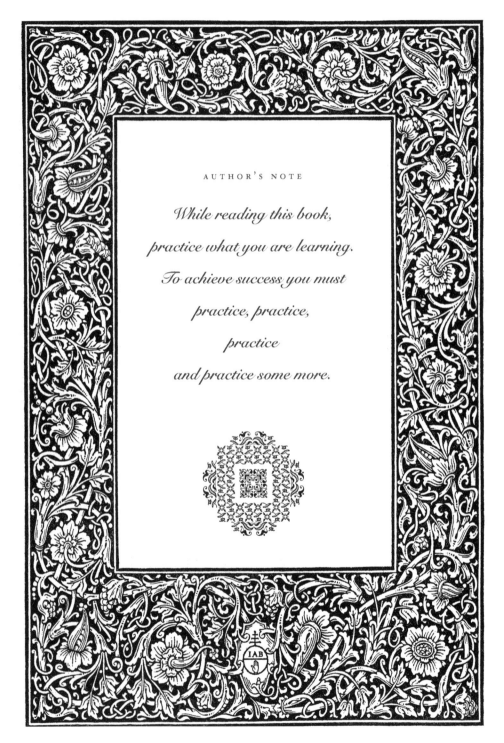

AUTHOR'S NOTE

*While reading this book,
practice what you are learning.
To achieve success you must
practice, practice,
practice
and practice some more.*

ACKNOWLEDGEMENTS

I offer my humble prostrations to my teacher, Sri Mata Amritanandamayi, also known as Amma (Mother), the Hugging Saint from Southern India, who gave me permission to put a picture of her hand in this book. After discussing several questions about lines in the hand, Amma looked at my hand, gave it a gentle squeeze, pointed to its fleshy mounts, and said, "the palm is a mandolin of consciousness." Thank you, Amma, for your unfathomable wisdom, being such a bright light on my path, and letting the readers of this book view your mystical palm.

Also, I want to thank my first palm reading teacher, Alta Kelly, who let me observe her while doing readings and gave me the encouragement to do this work. Importantly, I want to thank all of you who have trusted me to look into the mirror of your soul, and blessed me with amazing palm reading experiences that are too numerous to recount.

For all of you who spent your time reading my manuscript, I want to offer warm hugs of thanks. Especially I want to thank Nicola Scott and Lila Welchel for editing comments, Jude Simmons and Tara Daniels for help with art, and Mark Murphy for the design and layout and crafting these words into book form. And I can never thank Victor enough for his love and unfailing support.

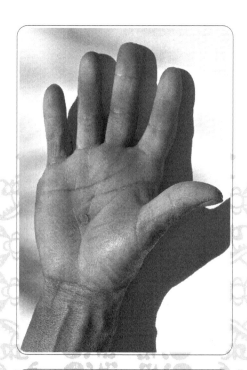
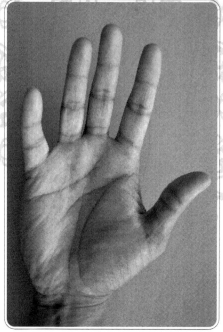

TABLE OF CONTENTS

Acknowledgements	5
Introduction:	
Mystical and Practical Elements of Palmistry	8
The Art of Palm Reading	9
Considerations Before You Begin	11
Preparing to Read the Hands	13
Chapter One: Getting Started	14
First Steps	15
When You Take A Person's Hand	16
The Flexibility Test	17
Reflections and Notations	18
Chapter Two: An Expression of Personality	22
First Contact: How To Begin Reading A Hand	23
What Do You Feel?	23
Skin Temperature:	
Determining The Predominant Element	24
What Do You See?	26
Reflections and Notations	29
Chapter Three: Using Astrology As A Foundation	
To Learn Palmistry	32
Entering The Esoteric World of Palmistry	33
Astrology and the Hand	33
Additional Astrological Sequences	37
The Fingers And Their Associated Planets	37
The Palm – A Cosmic Map of Consciousness	37
Reflections and Notations	41
Chapter Four: Reading The Fingers	44
Notice Details	45
The Most Common Finger Shapes	45
Finger Characteristics	50
Reflections and Notations	53
Chapter Five: The Thumbs and The Nails	56
Accessing The Thumbs	57
Some Characteristics Of The Thumb	58
Thumb Flexibility	59
Examining The Nails	60
Reflections and Notations	62

Chapter Six: Unveiling the Secrets in the Hand	64
Looking At The Palm	65
The Major Lines	65
Reflections and Notations	72
Chapter Seven: Estimating Age	
On The Major Lines And Line Variations	74
Determining Age On The Major Lines	75
Line Variations	76
Reflections and Notations	77
Chapter Eight: The Minor Lines:	
So Many Lines, So Little Time	80
Common Minor Lines	81
Signs and Symbols	85
Reflections and Notations	86
Chapter Nine: Your Passport To Success	88
Discussing The Most Popular Topics	89
Significant Characteristics of the Most Popular Topics	89
A Short Demonstration Reading of the Hand	91
A Little Pizzazz Goes A Long Way	92
Reflections and Notations	93
Chapter Ten: The Profit or The Prophet?	96
Effort Is Key	97
A Palm Reader's Code of Ethics	97
A Valuable Practice: Making Palm Prints	98
Reflections and Notations	102
Not To Be Missed Palmistry Classics	103
Notes	104
Bibliography	105
About the Author	106

INTRODUCTION

Mystical and Practical Elements of Traditional Palmistry

> *THE HAND IS THE TERMINAL PART OF THE HUMAN ARM CONTAINING THE PALM AND FINGERS...IT CONTAINS 27 BONES, 8 CARPALS, OR WRIST-BONES PROPER, 5 METACARPALS AND 14 PHALANGES — 3 TO EACH OF THE 4 FINGERS AND 2 TO THE THUMB.*

M.M. GAAFAR

THE ART OF PALM READING

Get comfortable and relax your mind for you are about to embark on a special journey that crosses from unchartered depths of the psyche into the mystic realm of foretelling events and doing character analysis through the study of the hand. Even if you don't intend to become a prognosticator and predict the future, once you tell someone that you are a palm reader you will be asked to reveal the secrets of what lies ahead in life, so be prepared. The best way to develop and strengthen your ability to answer questions about what lies hidden in the palm is to start building your hand analysis skills one day at a time. Let's begin now by learning some palmistry basics.

Conventional palmistry is a combination of two techniques: chirognomy, the study of the form and outer appearance of a hand; and chiromancy, the analysis of the lines and marks in the palm. This playbook provides a practical foundation of hand reading skills in relation to these two separate studies. Within its pages you'll find essential guidelines for examining various shapes, sizes and markings in the palm. As you put this information into practice, you will be on a path proven to increase hand analysis skills.

Discovering your own preferred method to read palms will result from interacting with numerous people and looking at their hands. Although you'll find guidelines for doing readings in these pages, becoming a palmist is only accomplished when you commit yourself to on-going practice. As you study various techniques in *The Art and Magic of Palmistry*, you will develop necessary skills and can decide what methods work best to create your personal hand reading style. While you are a beginning student, the choices you make in relation to your experiences will be your best teacher.

You might also be interested in learning one more hand reading method that does not require chirognomy or chiromancy. Another approach is the intuitive reading of the vibrations present in the hand. Some people can feel, see, or sense the energy, "chi", or the invisible essence of someone's soul personality in the hand and do a psychic reading based on this information. If you have this ability and use it, you will be considered a psychic palm reader. Even if you don't have this natural ability, with continual hand reading practice, you will automatically be learning to sense vibrations, and most likely you will increase your instinctive ability to do readings on this level. The palm is a focal point for learning to listen to and trust your intuition. As you do readings, your intuitive skills will naturally evolve. Just as when you exercise a muscle it gets stronger, your intuition becomes more developed as you repeatedly use it. Please keep an open-mind in relation to your own psychic development. "Beliefs about using your intuition open or close the door to using it effectively. To do so, you have to think its possible." (K. and V. Daniels in *Matrix Meditations*.)

This playbook will help you learn to recognize the most common characteristics you will encounter when looking at your own and other people's hands. It gives you guidelines to examine different shapes of the hand and the fingers, and to interpret the lines in the palm. In order to help simplify descriptive explanations, keywords are offered that can be used as prompts to help your studies. Keywords are a good starting place to train your mind in learning to interpret the palm. Once you've memorized essential terms for the various aspects of the hand, you will have built a practical foundation of information that you can use to help construct your readings. Don't underestimate the value of keywords, as they summarize the essential principles you need to understand in order to give a successful reading.

In this book you will also be shown the traditional placement of planets and zodiac signs on the hand, and be taught their significance in relation to understanding the personality. You don't have to be an astrologer to read the palm, but a little understanding of the zodiac can be beneficial for learning how to access personality traits.

To encourage you to put into practice the fundamentals you are being taught, you will encounter a question and answer section called "Reflections and Notations" at the end of every chapter. Please use the blank page spaces to create a journal to record the history of your experiences.

CONSIDERATIONS BEFORE YOU BEGIN

Having some general guidelines to follow can be helpful when you are first developing your skills. The following list contains ten suggestions for you to ponder and increase your chances to become a successful palm reader:

1. Find your extroverted, confident voice. Good communication is a must.

2. Take yourself seriously; yet look at your experience from a positive and upbeat point of view!

3. Smile when you're talking with someone about what you see in his or her hand. If you frown, the person will think that you're seeing something negative and become anxious.

4. Relax! If you make an assumption and your client says that it is incorrect, don't argue and try to convince the person that you are right. Sometimes even long-time professionals can read a line the wrong way.

5. Improve your chances for correct personality assessment by double-checking or cross-referencing your observations.

6. Develop a code of ethics to protect your client and yourself. An example can be found at the end of the book called, *A Palm Reader's Code Of Ethics*.

7. Don't push yourself to do more readings than you have the energy to do. Taking good care of yourself and use common sense to gauge how much energy you can share without becoming drained. If you find yourself weary after doing readings, sit in a bathtub with Epsom salts, and if possible, add fragrant herbs. An aromatherapy bath with mineral salts will surely help to re-energize you.

8. When you are first learning to read hands, consider what information would be valuable to you if you were the person receiving the reading. What questions might you want to ask a hand reader? Make appointments with other readers and have your palms read so that you can gain knowledge by watching how others read the hand.

{ CONTINUED }

CONSIDERATIONS BEFORE YOU BEGIN
{ CONTINUED }

9. Think about the message you are giving to your client in your discussion about what you see in his or her hand. The effect of your communication has the potential to greatly influence a person's psychological process and feelings and it contributes to your reputation as a reader.

10. To become a good palm reader, play the part well and act curious, courteous and professional.

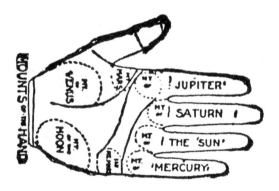

PALMISTRY TIP NO. 1

WHEN YOU ARE FIRST LEARNING HOW TO READ AND DISCUSS SOMEONE'S HAND, USE THE KEYWORDS THAT YOU FIND IN THIS BOOK. THEY ARE "SHORT CUTS" TO ASSIST YOU IN DEVELOPING YOUR PALMISTRY SKILLS.

PREPARING TO READ HANDS

*The following practices are optional, but they offer several preliminary procedures
for you to consider. Only follow the guidelines
if they make sense to you.*

You need to find a quiet space where you will not be disturbed. Before starting to do readings, one professional palmist always walks clockwise in a circle around her worktable. She throws salt on the ground to clear her space of other people's energy and keep unwanted vibrations from entering her space. Although you may not choose to do this practice, it's important for you to do whatever seems right to protect your space from intrusions. Other readers light candles and incense to help create a peaceful environment and set the mood for becoming receptive to symbolic messages in the palm of the hand.

Before you begin your work, it is important to clear your mind of psychic debris. You don't want to be thinking of what you're going to be having for dinner or how much you're hoping to see your lover when you start to do a reading. Unburden your mind as much as possible of restlessness or disturbing thoughts. Sometimes taking a few minutes to close your eyes, meditate, and focus on the rhythm of your breath can be calming. If you are spiritually minded, this is also a good time to say an invocation to the Great Spirit, or a prayer to your own personal guides, angels, or inner teachers, and ask for protection and guidance. You may want to perform a brief ritual to give thanks and ask the Divine Mystery to bless your work. For those who have this inclination your observance can involve a centering meditation:

*"Divine Infinite Light,
please connect my consciousness with the wisdom to accurately
read this person's hand."*

After you have completed any preliminary procedures of your choice, it's time to stretch and get comfy so you can begin your practice.

CHAPTER ONE

Getting Started

> *THE ELASTIC HAND – ONE WHICH RESISTS PRESSURE IN A LIVELY WAY, RATHER LIKE HARD, SPRINGY RUBBER – IS FOUND IN ACTIVE PEOPLE WHOSE ENERGY IS ABUNDANT AND FLOWS NATURALLY IN MENTAL AND PHYSICAL WORK.*
>
> FRED GETTINGS

FIRST STEPS

The most frequently asked question students typically ask about hand analysis is "How can I best learn palmistry?" Ultimately, each person chooses their own path of study, but for most people the best way to learn palmistry is to practice. Actually, when you think that you've practiced enough, it's almost time to practice some more. As a student it's important for you to remember to have fun as you examine hands and don't expect to answer every question you are asked during a palm reading. Your understanding of how to best answer questions will grow if you are determined to build your skills, are willing to practice, and are patient with your own learning process.

In order to become a successful palmist, you must be willing to ask both friends and strangers to look at their hands. Be tactful, gentle, and considerate when asking someone to enter their private world and view their palm. How a person offers you their hand is your first clue into his or her disposition. Is the person bold or shy about giving you his or her hand? Since both sides of the hand offer insight into the personality, you will want to inspect the complete hand.

You can ask to hold the hand(s) and have physical contact, or ask the person to merely show you his or her hand(s) and look without touching. You are responsible for choosing the palm reading technique that works most effectively for you. If you do your readings by holding a person's hand, always begin with a gentle touch as your initial contact with a person sets the tone for your involvement. Also while starting your practicing, be cheerful. Optimistic or positive communications will help you overcome any hurdles you might face.

Another popular question beginning students ask is "Which hand do I read?" When you are first learning to do this work, look at both hands and experiment with studying the lines on the right hand and compare how they are different from the left.

Before you begin to read palms, you must determine if you are going to analyze the right, left, or both hands. Let your instinct guide this decision. If you take the time to experiment with reading each hand and test different methods, you will get a sense of which one works best for you. What do you feel when you look at each hand? Which hand are you drawn to or naturally inclined to read?

In India, many palmists recommend reading a woman's left hand and a man's right hand. In the West, the popular gypsy method is reading the dominant hand in relation to a person's present efforts, their conscious awareness, and future potentials. In comparison, the less dominant or passive hand will be read as the past, inherited traits, or the subconscious personality. The dominant hand is the hand that is used most often, and usually the one that the person comfortably uses to eat, write, or throw a ball. The less active or passive hand is not the hand of choice to lift the fork, pen, hammer, etc. If a person is ambidextrous, meaning he or she uses both hands equally, you will need to study each hand to see which appears most physically developed and has the strongest lines. Trust your intuition as to which hand is most significant for your hand analysis. It's acceptable to look at both hands before you decide which hand should be read, or perhaps you will want to read both equally.

After you have developed your method for choosing which palm you will use to do your reading, and you have asked a person to give you his or her hand(s), you are ready to begin the next task. If you haven't already done so, it's time to follow the book's initial suggestion, (practice, practice, and practice some more), and directly experience what it feels like to examine the hand. Even a really good excuse as to why you can't practice (like having the flu) is only acceptable for a brief period of time.

WHEN YOU TAKE A PERSON'S HAND

Once you have a person's hand ready for observation, if you are holding the hand, you can gently perform the flexibility test (described below) to get your initial glimpse into personality traits. As a beginning hand reader, you will be developing your sense of the different ways that hands feel when they bend. After you have subtly tested flexibility in numerous hands you will have a much better understanding of how to compare and analyze the bendable range of motion. As with any other palm reading skills you are learning, give yourself time to practice so that you develop your insight to correctly access hand flexibility.

THE FLEXIBILITY TEST

The flexibility test is simple, yet revealing. When you first take a person's hand, carefully squeeze or bend back the entire hand including the fingers. Hands can be rigid and difficult to bend or very flexible and easy to bend. Perhaps a person's hand will be neither too stiff nor too limber, but somewhere in between these two extremes. The following keywords are a list of the character traits for the different ranges of hand flexibility you will encounter:

FLEXIBLE HANDS

These supple hands bend easily and feel relaxed when squeezed.
A flexible hand equals a flexible mind.

FLEXIBLE HANDS KEYWORDS

Adaptable, diplomatic, tactful, changeable, open to new ideas, willingness to compromise

---

RIGID HANDS

Rigid hands are stiff and feel hard to bend.
An inflexible hand points to an inflexible mind.

RIGID HANDS KEYWORDS

Stubbornness, overly cautious, obsessively disciplined, persevering, skeptical, dogmatic, or sometimes aloof

---

NEITHER FLEXIBLE NOR RIGID HANDS

Sometimes hands will feel neither flexible nor rigid when you squeeze them, but they will feel somewhere in between these two extremes.

NEITHER FLEXIBLE NOR RIGID HANDS KEYWORDS

Mentally versatile, personality can fit with most crowds, open minded—yet cautious, likes adventure—but not risk taking, takes the middle road in life

REFLECTIONS AND NOTATIONS : CHAPTER ONE

Please take time to contemplate and answer the following questions on a separate sheet or enter in your book. Please enter today's date:

Ask your friends if you can study their hands to help you learn to read palms. Make a list of people who you might you ask.

Do you feel ready to look at other people's hands? If your answer is "No." What do you need in order to feel comfortable and begin your actual study?

If you have begun your practice, what has been the most important insight you gained when looking at your own or someone else's hand?

Have you seen or sensed any differences between right and left hands?

Which hand do you want to read? Why?

What have you experienced when feeling flexible and rigid hands?

When looking at someone's hand what is your first reaction?

What does your gut instinct tell you about the person?

Record any memorable comments people made to you or your most significant reflections concerning your palm reading experiences:

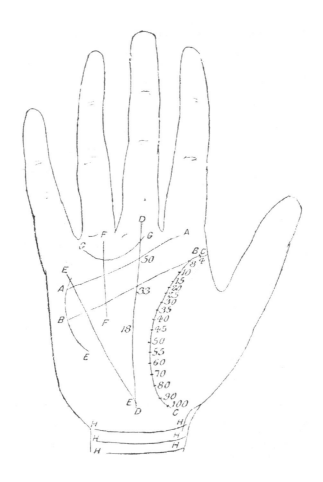

THE HAND AND ITS MARKINGS

A_A	LINE OF HEART	E_E	LINE OF HEALTH
B_B	LINE OF HEAD	F_F	LINE OF APOLLO
C_C	LINE OF LIFE	G_G	GIRDLE OF VENUS
D_D	LINE OF FATE	H_H	RASCETTES ENCIRCLE THE WRIST

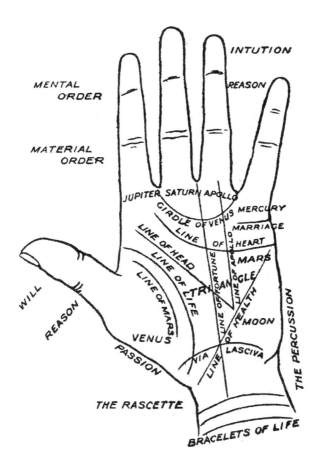

PALMISTRY TIP NO. 2

STUDY, STUDY, STUDY!

STUDY AS MANY HANDS AS YOU CAN TOUCH.

WHEN YOU LOOK AT SOMEONE'S HAND, SMILE AND BE CHEERFUL.

CHAPTER TWO

An Expression of Personality

> *THE SOFTER AND FINER THE SKIN,*
> *THE GREATER THE PHYSICAL AND EMOTIONAL*
> *SENSITIVITY…COARSE SKIN REFLECTS A MORE*
> *'ROUGH AND TUMBLE' INDIVIDUAL…*

NATHANIEL ALTMAN

FIRST CONTACT: HOW TO BEGIN READING A HAND

The open palm can be compared to a book that explores the potential of consciousness by telling a narrative of the trials and triumphs of a person's existence. For a palm reader, the hand and its lines portray an unfolding life story, and its unique markings are like arrows pointing to tendencies existing deep within. To be able to hear and understand the tone of each story, when you first take a person's hand you want to consider how it feels. Also notice if the person gives you their hand in an assertive or shy manner.

WHAT DO YOU FEEL?

When taking someone's hand, the skin is the first thing you touch. This remarkable part of the body will give you the first clue to understanding personality and temperament. The texture of the skin is distinctive in every hand.

SKIN TEXTURES
Smooth / Rough / In between Smooth and Rough

SMOOTH SKIN
Smooth hands are a sign of the use of skin lotion, luxury, or pampering. Smooth hands are also associated with work that mainly uses the mind, such as teaching, computing and legal professions.

ROUGH SKIN
When a person works hard with their hands, the skin can become dry, coarse, and more physically developed. The skin on hands of people who do physical work such as construction workers, mechanics and window washers, can show callous signs of being used in a rough environment.

SKIN TEMPERATURE: DETERMINING THE PREDOMINANT ELEMENT

SKIN TEMPERATURES
Moist / Dry / In between Moist and Dry

There are four predominant temperatures that you will feel in the palm: wet, hot, moderate, and cool. With practice, you will learn to measure variations within the range of these four qualities, from the oven hot hand to the palm that feels like a chilly wind. Most often the temperature in the hand can be linked with one of the four elements, earth, air, fire, and water. The following information can give you some understanding of how to determine personality traits from linking the noticeable temperature of the skin to one of the four elements:

WATER
Moist skin denotes the element water.

WATER KEYWORDS
Flowing emotions, imagination, intuition and sensitivity

You will find that some people have sweaty or wet palms. Moisture is an emotional indicator. The more water in a person's hand, the more emotions flow without restraint. When someone has a wet palm, it corresponds with strong feelings, passion, sensitivity, the intuition and a powerful imagination.

FIRE
Hot skin temperature indicates the element fire.

FIRE KEYWORDS
Fiery energy, creativity, passion, inspiration and excitement

Hot hands show excitement and enthusiasm for life, spirited communication, and active, fast mental energy. When you feel heat in someone's hand, it is a sign of strong feelings, warm affections, a fast temper, creative thinking and an assertive nature.

AIR
Moderate temperature on the palm denotes the element air.

AIR KEYWORDS

Inquiring intellect, dutiful, communicative and airy

An air hand is linked with a mind that likes to soar like the wind. This kind of hand is not too fleshy or hot, and not too cold. It corresponds with a balanced temperament, keen insight, practical ideals, and intellectual strength. But if the skin is rough or extremely dry, this hand temperature can also indicate impatience and a cautious, judgmental, or critical-minded nature.

EARTH
Cool skin temperature indicates the element earth.

EARTH KEYWORDS

Material minded, down-to-earth, practical and determined

The element earth is often represented by a combination of moderately cool temperature, a thick fleshy palm, and a rock-solid physical feeling in the way a person holds their palm. Earth energy is symbolic of strong security and financial needs, practicality, discrimination, and determination.

After you have done a flexibility test and felt for resistance or lack of resistance in hand flexibility, and have completed your scan of the hand for moisture and temperature, it is time to look more closely at the hand.

WHAT DO YOU SEE?

A simple place to begin your reading is to look at what is obvious! Simply look at the entire hand and closely study everything conspicuously visible.

NOTICE THE FOLLOWING PHYSICAL SIGNS:

a. Hand size
b. Bitten nails
c. Broken or dirty nails
d. Nail polish and/or fake nails
e. Brown spots on skin
f. Beauty marks
g. Scars
h. Tattoos
i. Jewelry

HAND SIZE
Look at the size of the hand in relation to the size of the body. A hand is only considered large if it is attached to someone with a medium or small sized body. Reversely, a hand is only considered small if it is attached to someone who has a medium-large or large body.

a. Small hands indicate determination, strength, and mental agility.
b. Large hands often point to a person who has large plans.

BITTEN NAILS
Usually the habit of chewing fingernails begins early in life. Perhaps the words "nervousness", "anxiety", and "stress" can be in your pool of adjectives to use when talking with the person who severely bites their nails.

BROKEN NAILS OR DIRTY HANDS
Broken nails indicate that a person is too busy to pay attention to the details of their physical appearance. However, sometimes a person will point out with embarrassment that one of their fingernails is broken and this comment demonstrates that he or she is self-conscious about their physical appearance. If dirt is in the nails or on the hand, look at what kind of dirt it is. If it is paint, the person may be an artist or has been recently occupied with painting a room or house. If marks are made with ink, the person may have been busy writing. If the dirt is just plain dirt, the person may

enjoy gardening or may have been doing yard work. Cross-reference these visible qualities in relation to other physical expressions of the hand (such as smoothness or callousness).

NAIL POLISH AND/OR FAKE NAILS

People who wear nail polish display their need to be attractive and fashionable. Self-esteem can be linked to concern for what others think about them. Those who wear dark colored polish are most often romantic and/or seductive by nature. If nail polish is chipped, it shows a lack of time to keep up with daily mundane chores. Extremely long painted, acrylic nails are often connected with idealism or a person who is very conscious of their sexuality.

BROWN SPOTS

In today's youth inspired world, facial cosmetic surgery can make it difficult to tell a person's age. Usually, the hands don't lie as they show tell tale signs of approximate age. If the brown spots on the backside of the hand are not beauty marks, they are most often liver spots that indicate a person is in their mature years. (A person's age is a factor in how you will discuss a person's life opportunities. Understandably, a young person will have different interests than a person who is looking at retirement in the near future. Age is one factor to help you gauge how to relate to your client.)

BEAUTY MARKS AND SCARS

Look at the location of any unusual markings. Once you understand the different associations with the specific areas of the hand (this is discussed in the chapter three), you can make comments in relation to beauty marks, cuts, or scars in comparison to where they appear on the hand. For instance, if a beauty mark sits on the area of the palm considered the Mount of the Moon you would discuss it in relation to lunar qualities. Also, look at the shape of the beauty mark or scar. Do they have any specific shape or qualities that has any symbolic associations? An example would be a scar that resembles the shape of an animal or a beauty mark that looks like a heart. It can prove valuable to discuss special markings in relation to their appearances and location on the hand.

{ CONTINUED }

WHAT DO YOU SEE?
{ CONTINUED }

TATTOOS

Tattoos on the hand are a symbolic link to the person's sense of identity. As the hand is the physical mirror that reflects the contents of the soul, any image that a person chooses to put on their hand is meaningful. What does the tattoo suggest in symbolic language? What associations do you have with the image? Tattoos can tell you a lot about the interests that a person identifies with and values held close to their heart. Below is a short list of examples of some symbols your might see on the hand or wrist and their potential significance:

SYMBOL	ASSOCIATION
A Dragon	Belief in magic and mysticism
Om symbol	Spiritual Interests
Tribal bands	Freedom Loving
Heart	Romance
Stars	Optimism

JEWELRY

What kind of impression does the person's jewelry make? Does it show a trendy personality, a conservative nature, or new age state of mind? Does a necklace or ring look like it could be a family heirloom? Is the jewelry set with expensive jewels such as diamonds or rubies, or molded glass or minerals? What finger is emphasized with a ring? For example, if a ring is worn on the finger of Mercury, emphasis is on Mercurial qualities. If a ring is worn on the wedding finger, chances are high that the person is married. Once you have experience reading many hands, you will increase your ability to analyze jewelry and its symbolic qualities in relation to the traits associated with the finger where the jewelry is being worn.

After you have checked for any distinctive marks or hand ornaments, it's time to become familiar with the overall characteristics of the hand. But before we begin our study of the most common shapes of the hand and finger types, we'll draw an invisible astrological blueprint on the palm to help guide you in determining personality characteristics.

REFLECTIONS AND NOTATIONS : CHAPTER TWO

Please take time to contemplate and answer the following questions on a separate sheet or enter in your book. Please enter today's date:

Imagine the hand you are looking at is able to talk. What does it want to tell you?

How many hands have you looked at since you began reading this text? How many palms have you looked at in the past week? Is your "field research" giving you enough practice to learn the ideas taught in this lesson?

At first glance, what do you want to examine when you are holding someone's hand?

Did you read enough hands to compare different skin textures and temperatures and their associated correspondences? What did you discover?

How would you describe the skin texture of your own hand?

{ CONTINUED }

REFLECTIONS AND NOTATIONS : CHAPTER TWO
{ CONTINUED }

How might you analyze your own hand to consider its dominant element? List keywords for your hand's dominant element.

Imagine that you are holding someone's hand that is hot to the touch, yet moist and sweaty. What are the personality keywords you would use to talk about these qualities?

Pretend you are looking at the hand of someone with severely bitten nails. What might you tactfully say to them about this trait?

Could you access any personality traits by looking at your own or some other person's jewelry?

Use the following space to record any memorable comments people made to you when you were practicing palmistry, and/or your most significant reflections concerning your hand reading experiences:

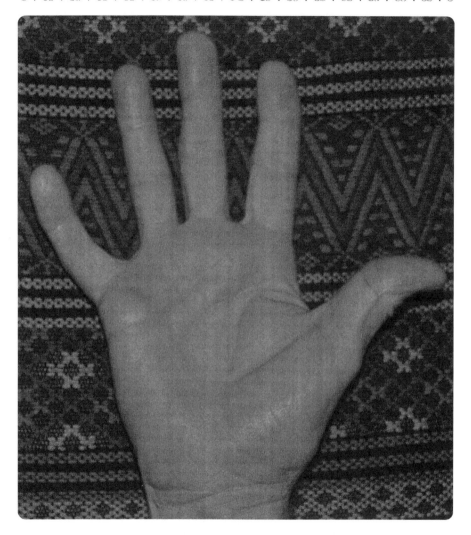

PALMISTRY TIP NO. 3

ASKING PEOPLE TO SEE THEIR HANDS GIVES YOU INSIGHT THAT ONLY EXPERIENCE CAN PROVIDE.

CHAPTER THREE

Using Astrology As a Foundation to Learn Palmistry

> "
>
> *WE DO NOT NEED ASTROLOGY.*
>
> *BUT IT IS AN EXQUISITE LANGUAGE BY WHICH*
>
> *TO BRING ALIVE ALL THE DIFFERENT FACETS*
>
> *OF OUR NATURES.*
>
> "
>
> CAROLINE W. CASEY

ENTERING THE ESOTERIC WORLD OF PALMISTRY

Before providing you specific details about hand reading, it is important to look at the correspondences between astrology and the palm. Although it is not required that you learn astrology to understand how to read the hand, this ancient science provides an underlying foundation of practical information to help you easily determine personality traits. Astrology is a primary root on the tree of divination, and even a basic understanding of astrology can enhance your palmistry practice.

As you follow the system in this book, you will learn correspondences between the palm and the zodiac. In this chapter, you will be shown the traditional placement of planets and Sun signs on the hand, and be taught their significance in relation to understanding the personality. This relevant information provides a virtual map of human characteristics overlaid on the palm that can help guide your hand reading discussions.

Please consider learning the following astrological basics, as you will be asked in this guidebook to incorporate them into future palm reading procedures. You do not have to learn all of this material in one day or one week; so don't become intimidated by the lists of zodiacal correspondences. Enjoy your learning process and put the different pieces of information together at your own pace, one step at a time.

ASTROLOGY AND THE HAND

If you haven't already studied horoscope interpretations, now is the time to learn some fun, simple "Sun sign" information. Most likely, you already know your Sun sign and read your daily horoscope in the newspaper. The Sun moves through twelve constellations as it goes around the earth in a year, and these are linked with the twelve zodiac signs. Your Sun sign is determined by whatever constellation the Sun was sitting in at the time of your birth. Each Sun sign is linked with a planet and one of the four elements. Their titles and important qualities are listed on the next page:

{ CONTINUED }

ASTROLOGY AND THE HAND

{ CONTINUED }

TWELVE SUN SIGNS	ASSOCIATED QUALITIES
1 Aries, the Ram	The Self, appearances
2 Taurus, the Bull	Material interests
3 Gemini, the Twins	Communication, travel
4 Cancer, the Crab	Mother, home
5 Leo, the Lion	Creativity, children
6 Virgo, the Virgin	Work, service, health
7 Libra, the Scales	Partnerships, marriage
8 Scorpio, the Scorpion	Death, sex
9 Sagittarius, the Archer	Philosophy, education,
10 Capricorn, the Goat	Ambitions, reputation
11 Aquarius, the Water Bearer	Community, friends
12 Pisces, the Fish	Subconscious, dreams

When looking at the fingers on the palm side of the hand, observe the spaces created by each separate phalanx or finger bone. (Each finger has three phalanges discernable by the spaces between the lines located over the joints on the fingers.) When doing traditional palmistry, each of these twelve phalanges and space it occupies corresponds to one of the twelve Sun signs. The planet alignments start with Aries on the top phalanx of the index finger, second phalanx is linked with Taurus, and Gemini occupies the bottom phalanx on this finger. Next, move to the top phalange of the Mercury finger for the location of the Sun sign, Cancer, and continue the zodiac sequence with each location being represented by the next phalanx. (Please see diagram showing the correspondences of Sun signs on fingers to the right.)

If you observe any unusual markings or characteristics in one of these twelve locations on the palm side of the fingers, mentally free associate potential symbolic meanings in relation to the keyword qualities of its corresponding Sun sign. Often, if one area has an unusual marking, it will signal an interesting connection to the Sun sign represented in this location.

{ CONTINUED }

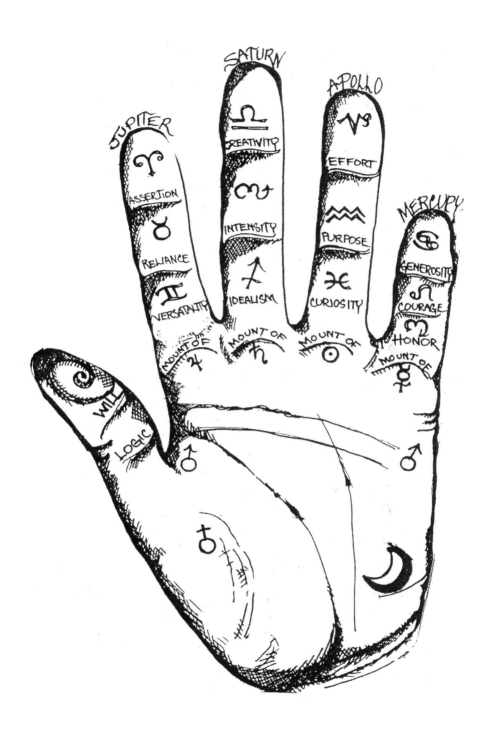

LOCATION OF PLANETS AND SUN SIGNS

ASTROLOGY AND THE HAND
{ CONTINUED }

Since every Sun sign is linked with a different element, knowing the connection between the signs and their associated elements—earth, air, fire, or water—may help you access the elemental qualities of the hand. In chapter two in the section titled Skin Temperature: Determining The Predominant Element the elements are explained in more detail. Relationships between signs and their corresponding elements are as follows: The zodiac fire signs are Aries, the forceful ram; Leo, the courageous lion; and Sagittarius, the aspiring archer. The practical earth signs are Capricorn, the determined goat; Taurus, the steadfast bull; and Virgo, the harvesting maiden. The sociable air signs are Libra, the balancing scales of justice; Aquarius, the expressive water bearer; and Gemini, the intelligent mutable twins. The emotional water signs are Cancer the domestic crab; Scorpio, the intuitive; and Pisces, the sensitive.

ADDITIONAL ASTROLOGICAL SEQUENCES

Are you ready to look at fingers in relation to astrology on the next level? If so, most likely you will be interested in the following zodiac correlations: The top phalanges on each hand are the cardinal signs of Aries, Cancer, Libra, and Capricorn. Cardinal energy is motivated, strong willed, and goal directed. The second, middle row of phalanges on each hand is the location of the fixed signs of Taurus, Leo, Scorpio, and Aquarius. Fixed signs are constant in their way of thinking, persistent, determined, and strongly motivated to rise to the top. The third, bottom row of phalanges relates to the mutable signs of Gemini, Virgo, Sagittarius, and Pisces. Mutable signs are linked with resilience, compromise, and high mental energy.

When looking at the length and thickness of the fingers, you can use this information to access which astrological quality is most dominant. At times when the phalanges seem equal size, the dominant quality may not appear obvious.

THE FINGERS AND THEIR ASSOCIATED PLANETS

Each finger corresponds to a different planet. In both hands, the index finger is linked to Jupiter, the planet that corresponds with leadership, ambition, philosophy, and fortune. The middle finger is associated with Saturn, linked with responsibility, work, discipline, karma, and seriousness. The ring finger is connected with the Sun and qualities of creativity, positive efforts, and fame. The little finger represents the planet Mercury associated with the powers of the intellect, communication, writing, travel, and health.

THE PALM – A COSMIC MAP OF CONSCIOUSNESS

Beneath each finger and the thumb are slightly elevated mounds of flesh called mounts. Each mount is related to a planet and its corresponding attributes. The mounts can be very large or high in size, moderately high, below average in height, or flat. The rule of thumb goes: the higher the mount, the greater the quantity of its corresponding planetary attributes. Reversely, when a mount is flat, you will attribute less importance to its planetary qualities. Most (but not all) of the mounts sit on the palm beneath the base of the fingers. Each mount that sits under a finger shares the name of the planet that rules its connecting finger.

{ CONTINUED }

THE PALM — A COSMIC MAP OF CONSCIOUSNESS
{ CONTINUED }

THE LOCATION AND NAME FOR EACH MOUNT

Mount of Mercury	Beneath the little finger.
Mount of the Sun	Beneath the base of the ring finger.
Mount of Saturn	Beneath the middle finger .
Mount of Jupiter	Beneath the Index finger.
Mount of Venus	At the base of the thumb.
Mount of the Moon	On the lower side of the outer edge of the palm opposite the thumb is the .
Lower Mars	Above the Mount of Venus between the index finger and thumb.
Upper Mars	The outside edge of the palm between the Mount of the Moon and the Mount of Mercury.
Plain of Mars	The area stretching across these two mounts in the middle of the palm.

As you can see from reading this chapter, if you put an overlay of astrological correspondences on the palm, it can play a significant role in helping you determine personality attributes. You can use basic knowledge of the zodiac, planets, and Sun signs to discuss universal human characteristics in relation to different points on the palm. The following keyword list acts as a brief reference guide to help you learn some of the meanings associated with the planets:

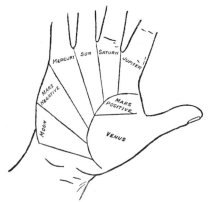

MOUNTS

The rule of thumb goes: the higher the mount, the greater the quantity of its corresponding planetary attributes.

38

SEVEN ANCIENT PLANETS AND CORRESPONDING MEANINGS

SUN

Associated with the Roman god of light and truth, Apollo
Linked with the Sun sign Leo

SUN KEYWORDS

Warm, sunny, positive energy; children; growth, creativity, happiness, vitality, leadership, willpower, and prosperity of spirit

MOON

Associated with Diana, Roman Goddess of the Moon and lunar energy
Linked with the Sun sign Cancer

MOON KEYWORDS

The subconscious, intuition, dreams, memory, reflection, imagination, emotions, empathy, moodiness, esoteric, travel, changes

MARS

Associated with Mars, Roman God of War
Linked with the Sun signs Aries and Scorpio

MOON KEYWORDS

Intense energy, quick action, physical drive, stamina, muscular strength, sexual vigor, will power, competition, assertiveness, courage, enthusiasm

VENUS

Associated with Venus, Roman goddess of fertility
Linked with the Sun signs Taurus and Libra

VENUS KEYWORDS

Beauty, harmony, love, desire, affection, passion, joy, social pleasures, recreational pursuits, music, poetry, drama, and the arts

{ CONTINUED }

SEVEN ANCIENT PLANETS AND CORRESPONDING MEANINGS
{ CONTINUED }

MERCURY

Associated with Roman god, Mercury, the messenger
Linked with the Sun signs Gemini and Virgo

MERCURY KEYWORDS

Ideas, mental alertness, discernment, analysis, critical perceptions, mental versatility, information, communication, writing, speech, travel

JUPITER

Associated with Roman god Jupiter, the protector
Linked with the Sun signs Sagittarius and Pisces

JUPITER KEYWORDS

Religion, philosophy, law, justice, wisdom, teaching, education, expansion, ambition, commerce, fortune, good will, generosity, foreign interests

SATURN

Associated with Roman god Saturn, and time of reaping
Linked with the Sun signs Capricorn and Aquarius

SATURN KEYWORDS

Karma, laws of cause and effect, lessons, time constraints, limitations, restrictions, responsibility, hard work, concentration, traditional values

REFLECTIONS AND NOTATIONS : CHAPTER THREE

Please take time to contemplate and answer the following questions on a separate sheet or enter in your book. Please enter today's date:

Why is it important to learn basic astrology when you are studying palmistry?

What is your Sun sign? What are some of the personality qualities for your Sun sign? Find the location on a finger that represents your Sun sign.

Make a finger map of the location of the twelve zodiac signs. List one or two keywords for each Sun sign.

If a client told you that her Sun sign was Scorpio, what planet would you talk about in relation to this sign?

{ CONTINUED }

REFLECTIONS AND NOTATIONS : CHAPTER THREE
{ CONTINUED }

Where do you locate the Sun sign, Taurus on the fingers? How might you talk about a Sun sign with your client?

What is a mount on the palm? Locate each mount and its associated planet on your own hand.

Name the seven ancient planets and list at least three keyword meanings for each one. What planet do you associate with each finger?

Use the following space to record any memorable comments people made to you when you were practicing palmistry, and/or your most significant reflections concerning your palm reading experiences:

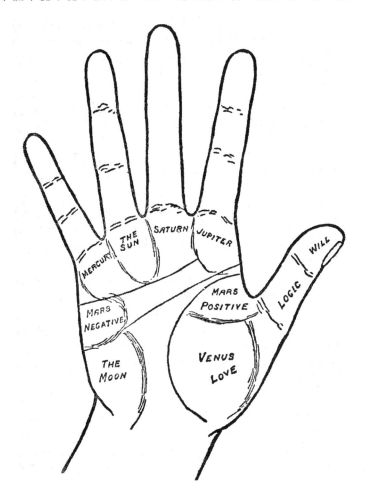

PALMISTRY TIP NO. 4

DON'T GET FATIGUED TRYING TO MEMORIZE ASTROLOGICAL DATA. IF YOU LEARN ITS BASICS IN MANAGEABLE BITS AND PIECES, EVEN A LITTLE UNDERSTANDING WILL BENEFIT YOUR READINGS.

CHAPTER FOUR

Reading The Fingers

> *DO NOT TRY TO CLASS ANY SET OF FINGERS IN A GROUP, BUT CONSIDER EACH ONE AND JUDGE IT BY ITSELF.*
>
> WILLIAM BENHAM

NOTICE DETAILS

When you first look at someone's hands, examine the entire shape of the hand and the fingers. As you study various hands, you will learn to determine the differences between hand and finger types. Of course, when someone gives you their hand, you will also notice the lines on the palm. Our study of specific lines comes later in chapter six.

THE MOST COMMON FINGER SHAPES

By learning the most common finger shapes, you will be well along your way to knowing how to discuss personality patterns in relation to finger types. Although there are many different finger shapes, the shapes that you will most often see are: spatulate, square, artistic, and the psychic, which is also called conic. At times, you will also see what is called the mixed finger hand, which is a combination of two or more of the various types of fingers. Less common finger types are the philosophic and the elementary. Below is a discussion of these universal finger shapes.

SPATULATE FINGERS (SHAPED LIKE A KITCHEN SPATULA)

The person who has spatulate shaped fingers is highly active and doesn't like being told what to do. He or she enjoys being the sole authority over their personal and career activities. A decision maker by nature, this person often assumes responsibility for organizing events and is steadfast in their focus on fulfillment of present or future goals.

SPATULATE FINGERS KEYWORDS

Original thinking, independent, mentally agile, enjoys taking the lead, contemplative, inquisitive, logical, determined, motivated, stable

THIS SHAPE WITH FLEXIBLE HAND

Open minded and willing to compromise

THIS SHAPE WITH INFLEXIBLE OR STIFF HAND

Needs structure, cautious

{ CONTINUED }

THE MOST COMMON FINGER SHAPES
{ CONTINUED }

SQUARE FINGERS (SQUARE IN SHAPE)

Common sense, a willingness to take responsibility, and efficiency makes the person who has the square or "useful" finger shaped hand invaluable in the work environment. Since pragmatism most often rules, these people will strive to get a job done on time or pay bills by their due date. They enjoy ruling the roost, but will usually make compromises when it comes to keeping other people happy and making peace in their home or work environment. Modest by nature, they can be quiet about their accomplishments and allow others to take the lead.

SQUARE FINGERS KEYWORDS

Practical, conventional, hard working, rational, materialistic minded, follows directions, strives to complete assigned tasks, domestic, needs security

THIS SHAPE WITH FLEXIBLE HAND

Willing to bend to other's demands

THIS SHAPE WITH INFLEXIBLE OR STIFF HAND

Stubbornness, unwilling to change easily

ARTISTIC FINGERS (MILDLY POINTED AT THE FINGER TIP)

Most often, feelings guide the perspective of a person who has artistic fingers. Usually sensitive by nature, this personality type will work to increase beneficial communications in the external world, or if angered, will minimally interact to maintain equilibrium and a positive flow of energy. Often, their focus is on using their creativity, or expressing themselves through some artistic medium. Enjoying life is essential to them, and they will often join in activities that focus on helping the planet in some way. Because their natural inclination is to make things better, the person who has these types of fingers values hope and good will.

ARTISTIC FINGERS KEYWORDS

Appreciates the arts, inspired, creative, imaginative, dreamy, sensual, listens to the heart more than the head, anti authoritarian

THIS SHAPE WITH FLEXIBLE HAND

Optimistic in finding the best solutions

THIS SHAPE WITH INFLEXIBLE OR STIFF HAND

Resistant to following the crowd

PSYCHIC (CONIC) FINGERS (VERY POINTED FINGER TIPS)

A person with psychic fingers has their inner eye searching for truth. Usually emotionally receptive, he or she can use just a little effort to develop their sixth sense. If the person is truly intuitive or psychic, he or she can be clairvoyant, clairaudient, or clairsentient, and will sometimes sense or see things that others won't. Not every person who has psychic fingers will believe that they have extra-sensory abilities. However, even if they don't believe in their psychic nature, most often they will have a trustable gut instinct about things. Frequently, this something extra enhances their common sense and the ability to read between the lines.

PSYCHIC FINGERS KEYWORDS

Intuitive, sensitive, emotional, ethereal, often practices spiritual disciplines or mystical arts, impressionable, idealistic, free spirited, needs privacy

THIS SHAPE WITH FLEXIBLE HAND

Expansive thinking, considerate of others

THIS SHAPE WITH INFLEXIBLE OR STIFF HAND

Disdains crowds, easy irritated or opinionated

{ CONTINUED }

THE MOST COMMON FINGER SHAPES
{ CONTINUED }

MIXED FINGER SHAPES (TWO OR MORE FINGER SHAPES ON ONE HAND)

The person who has a mix of different finger types will have a variety of personality characteristics that are represented by the combination of the specific finger types on their own hand. (Examine the fingers to see what type is most prominent.) People say that variety is the spice of life, and this saying certainly fits most who have mixed finger types. Also, love of life is a frequent characteristic of this person, who is inspired to make new friends and have soul stimulating communications. When seeking answers to serious questions about what will fulfill their love life or career path, their outward smiling nature will hide a tendency to be inwardly critical minded, restless, and not easily content.

MIXED FINGER SHAPES KEYWORDS

Worldly, versatile, changeable, able to see the value in diversity, energetic and usually understanding of different points of view

THIS SHAPE WITH FLEXIBLE HAND

Outwardly friendly, inwardly cautious

THIS SHAPE WITH INFLEXIBLE OR STIFF HAND

May be demanding or impatient

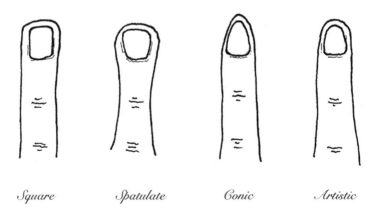

Square   Spatulate   Conic   Artistic

LESS COMMON FINGER TYPES

PHILOSOPHIC (LONG THIN FINGERS WITH KNOTTED JOINTS)

Although their personality can sometimes resemble the "absent minded professor", they will have an uncanny ability to rationalize about life in a thoughtful, philosophic manner. They can sometimes get lost in ideas that appear to reason out of range of the "normal" thinker. Because this person enjoys friendly, stimulating minds that encourage them to dive deeply into the mystery of life, they are often good communicators (unless they like to talk too much). However, sometimes they will appear aloof, as they can be quiet while they listen to others in order to seek the concealed meaning of what is being communicated.

PHILOSOPHIC KEYWORDS

Thoughtful, meditative, contemplative, academic, this person can get lost in their ideas and may appear intellectually aloof

THIS SHAPE WITH FLEXIBLE HAND

Compromising and thought provoking

THIS SHAPE WITH INFLEXIBLE OR STIFF HAND

Opinionated with a strong moral sense

ELEMENTARY FINGERS (EXCEPTIONALLY THICK SQUARE FINGERS, WIDE THUMB)

Fat, thick fingers can sometimes relates to over indulgence, and the quest to fulfill insatiable desires or hedonistic tendencies. You may find that the person who has this finger type is easily frustrated if life isn't to their liking. If he or she is upset, their feelings may boil over like a pot cooking on the stove, and they might not be shy in letting you know what is wrong. Also, if the entire hand is extremely thick, the person may not have social etiquette, or be sensitive to other's emotional needs. They can also be promiscuous or overly flirtatious. When combined with strong physical energy, they can be athletic or military minded, and do well forging ahead where others fear to tread.

ELEMENTARY FINGERS KEYWORDS

Passionate, controlling, self-centered, over indulgent, easily irritated, sometimes offensive because there can be a lack of consideration

THIS SHAPE WITH FLEXIBLE HAND

Socially outgoing, a potential party animal

THIS SHAPE WITH INFLEXIBLE OR STIFF HAND

Stubborn with unbendable will

FINGER CHARACTERISTICS

LONG FINGERS

Long fingers are called such when the fingers are longer than the length of the palm itself. The people who have long fingers are most often original thinkers who do not like people telling them what to think or do. If fingers are exceptionally long, the person is most often motivated to lead others or instigate a worthy cause.

In relation to individual fingers, if the finger of Mercury appears exceptionally long, the qualities of Mercury will be pronounced. When Apollo is longer than the finger of Jupiter, creativity will be more important than leadership. Whereas if the finger of Jupiter is longer than the finger of Apollo, the desire for power and leadership will be more central in a person's life than the desire to use their creativity. An exceptionally long finger of Saturn is linked with responsibility, hard work, and a serious disposition. Also, it can indicate that a person may be a workaholic or in some way married to their career.

LONG FINGERS KEYWORDS
Contemplative, thoughtful, intellectual, diplomatic, cautious,
enjoys organizing and making plans, self-reliant

SHORT FINGERS

Short fingers on a person's hand means that the fingers are shorter or no longer than the length of the palm. Characteristically, people with short fingers are human dynamos with lots of energy to accomplish whatever task is at hand. They may work patiently on projects, but may become restless if projects carry on too long, as they tend to like to get things done and move on to the next opportunity. If they seem to be in a hurry, it's because they usually are.

SHORT FINGERS KEYWORDS
Curious, quick thinking, adventurous, may be impatient with others
who don't a share similar vision.

SMOOTH FINGERS (WITHOUT PROTRUDING KNUCKLES)

People who have smooth fingers are often team players, friendly, and can get along with most personality types. Although the people who have these finger types may look strong, often the beauty in the smooth skin type and bone structure disguises a fragile or changeable emotional nature. People who possess such fingers stay happy by being productive and are often willing to go the extra distance to make a good impression.

SMOOTH FINGERS KEYWORDS

Impulsive, temperamental, fashionable, security conscious, helpful to others

KNOTTY FINGERS (WITH PROTRUDING KNUCKLES)

Thick and bumpy knuckles are characteristic of the knotty finger. People who have knotty fingers can easily ignore practical reality such as the need to do housework in favor of more important philosophic or lofty ideals. Some who have this finger type are emotionally quiet, as the inner world of ideas is their playground of choice. Sometimes feelings may be overlooked as a way to escape dealing with something they often find not so easy to understand.

KNOTTY FINGERS KEYWORDS

Analytical, philosophical, quick minded, reflective, orderly, systematic, depth of understanding

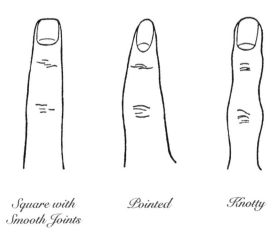

Square with Smooth Joints   *Pointed*   *Knotty*

NATURALLY BENT FINGERS (FINGERS THAT LEAN SIDEWAYS)

If a finger is bent, observe how much it is bent and what direction it points. The more a finger bends, the more out of the ordinary are the normal attributes or qualities associated with this finger.

If fingers bend toward the thumb, it can indicate social or extroverted qualities. When fingers bend toward the little finger (finger of Mercury), it can represent an introverted nature.

NATURALLY BENT FINGERS KEYWORDS
Attributes are characterized in relation to qualities of specific finger

When the finger is bent only slightly, there is only a slight alteration for the normal meaning of this finger. If the finger is curved in a pronounced or twisted manner, it puts a greater focus on an out-of-the-ordinary trait in relation to the qualities normally associated with the bent finger. Finger qualities may be altered in relation to a crooked finger in ways such as those listed below:

FINGERS	BENT FINGER QUALITIES
Little finger (Mercury)	Communication strong point or obsession with writing or health
Ring finger (Apollo)	Creativity—may be stifled or too much emphasis on fame and fortune
Middle finger (Saturn)	Seriousness or work may overrule fun
Index finger (Jupiter)	Leadership and ambition may be strong forces to reckon with

REFLECTIONS AND NOTATIONS : CHAPTER FOUR

Please take time to contemplate and answer the following questions on a separate sheet or enter in your book. Please enter today's date:

Did you notice anything unusual about the fingers of the hands you examined? If yes, what did this uncommon quality represent to you?

List the different finger shapes. What human attributes correspond to each finger type?

How do you classify your own finger shapes? What does this say about you?

What would you tell someone who has knotted joints on their index finger?

{ CONTINUED }

REFLECTIONS AND NOTATIONS : CHAPTER THREE
{ CONTINUED }

What are the qualities associated with the little finger? What would you say about a little finger bent toward the ring finger?

What might you tell someone who has lost one or more fingers?
(Hint: What planet rules the missing finger?)

Besides your middle finger, what is your longest finger?
What does this say about you?

Use the following space to record any memorable comments people made to you, or your most significant reflections concerning your palm reading experiences:

PALMISTRY TIP NO. 5

CALM AND CENTER YOUR INNER SELF
TO ENABLE YOUR MIND TO FOCUS AND FINE-TUNE ITS OBSERVATION OF
WHAT LIES IN SOMEONE'S HAND.

CHAPTER FIVE

The Thumbs and The Nails

"

THE MAN WITH THE SHORT, CLUMSY, THICK-SET THUMB IS COARSE AND BRUTISH IN HIS IDEAS AND ANIMAL IN HIS INSTINCTS, WHILE THE MAN OR WOMAN WITH THE LONG, WELL-SHAPED THUMB IS INTELLECTUAL AND REFINED, AND IN THE ATTAINMENT OF A DESIRE, OR THE CARRYING OUT OF AN OBJECT, SUCH A PERSON WILL USE THE STRENGTH OF INTELLECTUAL WILL, AS OPPOSED TO THAT OF BRUTE FORCE, WHICH WILL BE APPLIED BY THE MAN WITH THE THICK, SHORT FORMATION.

"

CHEIRO

ACCESSING THE THUMBS

Thumbs come in various sizes and shapes. They can be straight or curved and the curves can be slight or significant. Many hand readers agree that the angle and shape of the thumb indicates the nature of the personality. When you study the thumb, you will notice that it is divided into three sections: the top, the middle, and the bottom. The top phalanx, represents will power and strength of mind; the middle phalanx, is linked with logic and reasoning abilities; and the thumb's base is called the Mount of Venus, which corresponds with love, family, and emotional sensitivity.

The general rules of reading the thumb are as follows: the wider and longer the thumb, the more extrovert and willful the personality; and the narrower and shorter the thumb, the more cautious the personality. For example, a large Mount of Venus indicates a passionate nature, while a flat Mount of Venus is a sign of emotions held in check. If the middle of the thumb (the middle phalanx) is long and large, it may represent active or commanding logical tendencies, whereas if the middle of the thumb is small and short, it can indicate a passive logical nature (a person who doesn't assert their ideas). If the top section of the thumb (the top phalanx) is long and large, it suggests strong will power, whereas if it is short and small, it implies a more bendable will.

Please note that when analyzing a thumb, you would not base your evaluation of its size by comparing it with the thumb on some other person's hand. Instead, make your comparison by examining the different shapes and sizes apparent on the three sections on one thumb on one hand.

Top phalange larger than middle

Middle phalange larger than top

Middle phalange larger than top

SOME CHARACTERISTICS OF THE THUMB

TOP PHALANGE LARGER THAN MIDDLE PHALANGE

KEYWORDS

Willful, determined, makes large plans, assertive, ardent in pursuing goals, tends to be strong-minded and take control

MIDDLE PHALANGE OF THUMB LARGER THAN TOP PHALANGE

KEYWORDS

Guided by reason, takes time to consider alternatives instead of jumping into decisions, willing to compromise

A FAT, THICK THUMB

KEYWORDS

Stubborn, skeptical of the unfamiliar, resists change or new ideas, may ignore protocol, strongly opinionated, aggressive

A NARROW THIN THUMB

KEYWORDS

Critical minded, wishful, bends to the demands of others; impatient, holds feelings in check despite strong emotional tendencies

THE STRAIGHT THUMB

KEYWORDS

Strongly goal minded, dogmatic, straight to the point, reaches for the stars, idealistic, energetic, independent thinking

THE ARCHING THUMB (RESEMBLES A CRESCENT MOON)

KEYWORDS

Dynamic, expressive, sentimental, nurturing, open-minded, willing to change, insightful, pays attention to gut instincts

THUMB FLEXIBILITY

When you examine the hand to determine if it is flexible or rigid, remember to also examine the flexibility of the thumb. You can try this simple, yet valuable test just before you consider the merits of the thumb: gently bend the thumb to determine if the middle joint is able to bend or if the thumb is too stiff to bend at this point.

STIFF THUMB (HARD TO BEND AT JOINT)

A rigid thumb can indicate that the person enjoys extending the power of their ideas and making an impact.

KEYWORDS

Willful to the point of being stubborn, inflexible, determined, self-reliant, analytical, observant, sensible, cautious, frugal

FLEXIBLE THUMB (EASY TO BEND AT JOINT)

When the thumb bend easily and is soft to the touch, there may be an external willingness to bend to life's circumstance. Instead of a demanding personality, the people with this thumb type may concede their power to those who are strongly persuasive.

KEYWORDS

Bends to people's demands, adaptable, mentality flexible, diplomatic, dogmatic, compromising, wants to please

---

EVALUATE THROUGH COMPARISON

When determining personality traits such as willpower in relation to the thumb size, cross-reference the accuracy of your interpretation by evaluating the height of the Mount of Mars. If Mars is high, this reaffirms a strong assertive nature. If the Mount of Mars is flat, a person may be less inclined to assert their will.

EXAMINING THE NAILS

Fingernails can be shiny or dull, long or short, clean or dirty, filed and painted, or bitten nervously. When you consider fingernails, look for signs that will give you clues to personality traits. For instance, if all the nails are uncommonly thin and splitting, there may be a lack of proper diet or too much stress. Bitten nails equal nervousness. Polished nails are linked with being fashion minded or concerns about what other people think when they look at you.

The following is a short list for you to contemplate:

NAIL CHARACTERISTICS	POTENTIAL MEANING
Shiny, natural color	High energy
Dull, natural color	Low energy
Long nails	Fashion statement
Short nails	Practical nature
Brittle nails	Health or dietary concerns
Clean nails	Concerned about appearance
*Dirty nails	Lack of concern about physical appearances.

* *If the dirt is ink or paint, this may be a clue about hobbies or professional interests.*

BASIC NAIL SHAPES

NARROW NAIL

Impatience often accompanies a person who has small set nails. Their mind moves fast to accomplish goals and extend personal boundaries. Dreams play an important role in lifting their ordinary reality toward celestial spheres of creative, philosophical, or spiritual objectives.

They fight boredom with every ounce of intelligence to keep life moving quickly toward adventure in worldly experience. Thin and narrow nails can also indicate the type of person who prefers to avoid the practical world and keeps his or her head in the mystical realm.

NARROW NAIL KEYWORDS
Quick thinking, curious, opinionated

MEDIUM NAIL WIDTH

When the nail has a medium sized base, you might be meeting someone who is skeptical about what you are doing. Thinkers by nature, these people will analyze, try to determine the outcome, or prejudge the value of whatever they are involved with, even before the dice have been tossed to see who wins the game of life. Their minds often rule over the wisdom of their hearts, and they can make hasty decisions.

MEDIUM NAIL WIDTH KEYWORDS
Inquisitive, enjoys debate, observant

WIDE NAIL BASE

The person who has a wide nail base likes to keep track of financial and common sense, practical matters. Finding the right path to material success will usually become a high priority and motivating force. Even-tempered and often fair-minded, they enjoy walking the middle path to stay secure and improve their chances for reaching their goals.

WIDE NAIL BASE KEYWORDS
Physically strong, practical, candid

FLUTED OR RIPPLED NAIL

Fluted nails look like an old fashion washboard with ripples going across the base in a vertical direction. This nail shape is connected with an active Mercurial nature, associated with over analysis, nervousness, and anxiety. The person may have a hard time relaxing or may not sleep well. Access the thickness of the base of the finger in order to best determine how the qualities of the fluted nail will be represented. For example, if a person has a narrow nail base and it is also fluted, you would discuss rippled qualities in relation to personality qualities connected with a person being quick thinking, curious, and opinionated. If a person has a wide nail base, you would talk about fluted qualities such as nervousness or defensiveness in relation to physical strength, practical mindedness, and consideration of others.

FLUTED OR RIPPLED NAIL KEYWORDS
Nervous, defensive, or high-strung

REFLECTIONS AND NOTATIONS : CHAPTER FIVE

Please take time to contemplate and answer the following questions on a separate sheet or enter in your book. Please enter today's date:

Did you notice anything unusual in the thumbs on the hands you studied? What qualities did you observe and what did these represent to you?

What is the difference between a thumb that bends easily and one that is stiff?

Describe the angle and characteristics of your own thumbs.

What part of hand is called the Mount of Venus? What does this mount represent if it is high or apparently low?

What was most interesting to you when you were looking at your own and other people's nails?

Would you classify the shape of your nails as narrow, medium wide, or wide? What are the characteristics of these types of nails?

Examine your own hand, and answer this frequently asked palm reading question: "Will I be successful in my future?"

Use the following space to record any memorable comments people made to you, or your most significant reflections concerning your palm reading experiences:

PALMISTRY TIP NO. 6

THERE'S ALWAYS A LOT GOING ON INSIDE A PERSON THAT'S INVISIBLE TO OUTSIDERS. NEVER UNDERESTIMATE THE STRENGTH OF WHAT LIES BENEATH THE SURFACE.

CHAPTER SIX

Unveiling the Secrets in The Hand

THE IDEA THAT THE LINES OF THE HAND ARE INTIMATELY CONNECTED WITH THE PSYCHE IS, OF COURSE, AS OLD AS PALMISTRY ITSELF.

FRED GETTINGS

LOOKING AT THE PALM

Now it's time to start to pay close attention to the major lines in the palm, and where each begins and ends. You will want to look at the size, shape, length, depth, color, and any unusual feature of each line. Pay attention to any mark within a line that is out of the ordinary, as unusual markings are red flags for special occurrences. Unusual markings will need to be considered in relation to their symbolic nature (determined by the mark's shape, size, and appearance). You should no longer look at each line only as a line (palmistry scholar William Benham refers to them as "life maps"). It becomes important to see each line as a flow of energy that represents some aspect of personality or potential life direction.

The level of vitality in a line is determined by the strength or absence of its appearance. These lines will give you insight into the innate nature of the hand owner's personality. Only through comparison of lines on a variety of different hands is it possible to gain understanding of the potential diversity of these major lines. Ultimately, it is the experience of viewing numerous hands that will be the best guide to help you make comparisons concerning the range of possibilities for each line.

THE MAJOR LINES

There are four major lines on the palm. Each represents a specific aspect of consciousness. The major lines represent core qualities in life, love, career or fate, and the mentality. The major lines are usually the longest lines on the palm.

You will usually find these principal lines on every hand, but don't worry if occasionally you see a hand that lacks a major line. For example, some people may not have a Career Line, or they may only have a partial Love Line. Remember that every person has a unique hand, and no two hands will show the same features. This uniqueness factor is what makes palmistry so interesting. It is up to you, the palmist, to determine which lines and marks are most significant in determining personality characteristics.

{ CONTINUED }

THE MAJOR LINES
{ CONTINUED }

When you are looking at major lines, you will sometimes see forked lines, breaks, double or parallel lines, fraying ends or beginnings, or multiple tiny, fine lines leading into the main line. Line variations such as these are discussed in more detail in chapter seven, "Minor Lines".

THE LIFE LINE

The Life Line or Line of Vitality is one of the longest lines on the palm. It starts somewhere between the index finger and the thumb and extends in a curve along side the outside edge of the Mount of Venus all the way toward the wrist. This line corresponds to significant life circumstances and activities. It represents the flow of energy or chi, and a break in a line suggests a rupture, disturbance, or change in the force of life energy.

Many times when there is a break in this line, people think that they have a short Life Line and fear their life will be short. It is important to note that a break in the line does not mean that life is going to end suddenly which many people incorrectly assume. If you observe another line that begins shortly after the break in the Life Line, and it continues in the same direction as a typical Life Line, it is considered a continuation of this same line. Often, after a break in the Life Line, a continuing line will parallel the original line but may be closer to or farther away from the thumb.
When the Life Line is close to the thumb it indicates a person who is interdependent on the family. When this line extends away from the Mount of Venus toward the Mount of the Moon it indicates greater emotional independence.

Many people will ask you when they are going to die in relation to the length of their Line of Life. Some palmistry books claim that the longer this line, the longer the life, and the shorter this line, the shorter the life. Studies have been performed in mortuaries that prove this theory to be incorrect. A short Life Line can represent that a person has a low energy level, or that they will be making a significant life change.

My suggestion for inquiries such as "How long am I going to live?" is to tell people that the length of the line doesn't refer to the length of life, but to vitality and how much life you put into your living. Palm readers are not omniscient, and therefore shouldn't suggest the time for a person's death. If a person is overly stressed about a short Life Line, you can tell them to discuss their longevity concerns with their doctor.

THE LIFE LINE KEYWORDS
Vitality, life plans, purpose, important events, life transitions

THE LIFE LINE — LINE BEGINNINGS

If the highest point of the Life Line begins high on the palm somewhere inside the Mount of Jupiter (beneath the index finger), it suggests a life filled with powerful efforts, ambitions, and exacting abilities that can affect success in life.

When the beginning of this line is located half way between the thumb and the index finger, it represents a life force that is energetic and motivated to win.

Though rare, if a Life Line starts at the base of the thumb, Mars fiery energy will be entwined with the life force.

THE LIFE LINE — LINE ENDINGS

The end of the Life Line suggests energy level, activities, and efforts during the later part of life. The most common place for this line to end is near the wrist. When it curves under the Mount of Venus and actually reaches the wrist, a person has an extremely strong emotional life current, and the needs for family or loved ones will be consuming. But if it goes straight down toward the wrist without curving under the Mount of Venus, the life is filled with activities that lead to fulfillment of personal goals (with less of a strong focus on family).

When the bottom of the Life Line extends across the palm and travels toward the Mount of the Moon, life efforts are expansive, adventurous, changeable, and often times unconventional.

LOVE LINE

The Love Line, also called the Heart Line and Line of Romance, is one of the most important lines in the hand. After all, nearly everyone wants to know about his or her love life. Understanding how to talk about this line is a prerequisite for becoming a palm reader. If the line is long, it is considered a sign of a passionate emotional nature. A longer line indicates stronger inclinations to communicate about feelings or discuss matters of the heart.

THE LOVE LINE KEYWORDS

Affections, emotions, jealousy, heart commitments, anything that touches the heart

THE LOVE LINE — LINE BEGINNINGS

The beginning of the line (located somewhere on the thumb side of the hand on the upper third of the palm) is regarded as the beginning stages of the love life. If it's located in the middle of the Mount of Jupiter, a person may have high ideals, ambitions, and expectations about love and fulfillment.

If the beginning of the line runs all the way to the top of the hand where the finger of Jupiter begins, it is a sign of good luck in love as Jupiter is associated with good fortune.

When the beginning of this line starts under the middle finger—the finger of Saturn—it signifies a lack of willingness to discuss emotions, or an emotionally serious nature. The shorter the Love Line, the less willing a person is to disclose their feelings. Often times, a person with a Love Line that begins in the Mount of Saturn will need to be drawn out in conversations of a romantic nature.

If the beginning of this line begins close to the Head Line, emotions will be controlled by the intellect. Most likely, the person will be overly analytical about their feelings.

THE LOVE LINE — LINE ENDINGS

The end of this line, located somewhere beneath the little finger and Mount of Mercury, can be deep or shallow and may or may not have fraying lines. A clear, straight ending to this line indicates satisfaction in love. If this part of the line has many little fine lines, however, the person's emotions may loose some strength through worry or insecurity.

If this line ends on or near the Mount of Mars, a person may be emotionally stubborn or assertive in communications with their loved ones.

CAREER, FATE OR LINE OF DESTINY

This line illuminates the direction of a person's career or fate. Some hands will lack this line. If the palm does not have a line of destiny, it most often suggests a person who will move through life with uncertainty about career choices or feel that they can't find their calling. Career choices may not be easily defined.

CAREER, FATE OR LINE OF DESTINY KEYWORDS
Fortune, career, goals, opportunities, success

CAREER, FATE OR LINE OF DESTINY — LINE BEGINNINGS

This line usually starts somewhere in the area near the wrist and travels upward through the middle of the hand toward the fingers. (Less frequently, you may find this line starting somewhere near the middle of the palm.)

If the Career Line begins anywhere near the Mount of the Moon, the person's life will take on qualities associated with this mount (imagination and intuition), and the person will be creative in their career choice. Usually, they won't like routine, convention, or traditional professions. Such people are often free-spirited by nature.

If this line starts at the base of the hand near the wrist and is in the center of the palm (equidistance from the Mount of the Moon and Mount of Venus), a person is comfortable walking life's middle path. They will be a team player, or feel at home in corporate environments, or make choices that fit within traditional or corporate work values.

{ CONTINUED }

CAREER, FATE OR LINE OF DESTINY — LINE BEGINNINGS
{ CONTINUED }

If the Career Line starts anywhere on the Mount of Venus (toward the base of the thumb), a person's fate is tied to family demands and expectations. Love will have a strong influence on career choices.

If it starts high in the middle of the hand, somewhere near the Head Line, a person will often take a long time to determine the direction they want to go in career.

CAREER, FATE OR LINE OF DESTINY — LINE ENDINGS

The end of this line is most often located somewhere in the top half of the palm. Most often it ends in the Mount of Saturn or Mount of Jupiter. When the Career Line ends within the Mount of Saturn, a person will work hard to attain their goals. Personal responsibility and effort is the key to success and accomplishment.

Sometimes the Career Line goes toward the Mount of Jupiter. This type of Career Line will be linked with the qualities of strong ambition, leadership, philosophy, and expansiveness.

If a person has a partial Career Line and it only goes as high as the middle of the palm, it is a sign that the person may need to work hard to create a vision for the future. Or, perhaps they may retire early and not need to work in their later life.

Major Lines
LOVE, FATE, HEAD, LIFE

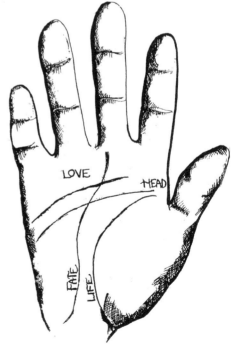

HEAD LINE OR LINE OF MENTALITY

The Head Line represents mental qualities. It can either be a straight or somewhat curved horizontal line across the middle of the palm. It begins on the thumb side of the hand. If it's a short line, it ends somewhere near the middle of the palm, and if it's a long Head Line, it ends near the outside edge of the palm.

HEAD LINE OR LINE OF MENTALITY KEYWORDS

Concentration, common sense, decision- making, intelligence, concentration, ability to focus

HEAD LINE OR LINE OF MENTALITY — LINE BEGINNINGS

Sometimes the beginning of the line is entwined with the beginning of the Life Line. Simply stated, when these two lines are connected, it represents a life governed by reason and logic. When these two lines have space between them at their starting location, it indicates a person who lives spontaneously or doesn't take a long time to make decisions.

If the beginning of this line starts in the Mount of Jupiter, a person will be motivated to study and excel at gathering knowledge.

HEAD LINE OR LINE OF MENTALITY — LINE ENDINGS

When the Head Line is short and ends in the middle of the hand, it represents a person who is linear minded, a matter-of-fact thinker who sticks to facts. The longer the line, the more time a person will need to analyze, deliberate, and make decisions. When the end of the line sits on the Mount of Mars, it suggests a more assertive and fiery mentality. If this line curves downward toward the Mount of the Moon, it usually indicates someone who has a lunar or strongly emotional and imaginative temperament.

Note: The horizontal space between the Head Line and the Love Line is called the Quadrangle. It's the space where the head and heart come together and it represents the balancing point between the mind and the emotions. A narrow Quadrangle indicates a lack of emotional trust. A wide Quadrangle represents a warm-hearted outlook.

REFLECTIONS AND NOTATIONS : CHAPTER SIX

Please take time to contemplate and answer the following questions on a separate sheet or enter in your book. Please enter today's date:

Did you notice anything unusual about any major line(s) when you took someone's hand, or looked at your own hand? What did this uncommon quality represent?

What are the different major lines? What attributes correspond to each of these lines?

Explain the qualities of the Life Line.

Look at your own Life Line. What does its ending direction tell you about yourself?

What might you tell someone who has a short Life Line?

What might you tell someone who has a missing Career Line?

What is the difference between a Line of Mentality and a Head Line?

Use the following space to record any memorable comments people made to you, or your most significant reflections concerning your palm reading experiences:

PALMISTRY TIP NO. 7

EXPERIENCE IS YOUR BEST TEACHER.

CHAPTER SEVEN

Estimating Age On the Major Lines and Line Variations

> *...THE IDEA HERE IS NOT TO DWELL ON THE PAST, EITHER IN THIS LIFE OR IN PAST INCARNATIONS, BUT ON HOW CONSCIOUS WE ARE. AFTER ALL, WE NEED TO LIVE AND WORK IN THE PRESENT. THIS IS WHERE OUR EVOLUTION TAKES PLACE.*
>
> GHANSHYAM SINGH BIRLA

DETERMINING AGE ON THE MAJOR LINES

Although you may recognize an event's date of occurrence anywhere on the palm, estimating age for specific actions is most often done on the major lines. By following your intuition and the guidelines described below you'll be using a system for measuring time that was established long ago in the early history of palm reading. General rule of measurement for an adult average size hand is a half-inch on a line equals about ten years of time. Please see the palm diagram on pg. 20 for age approximations on the various lines.

ESTIMATING AGE ON THE LIFE LINE

The beginning of a person's life is denoted at the point where the Life Line begins between the thumb and the index finger. The last stage in life is read at the bottom of this line usually where it intersects or nearly meets the wrist.

ESTIMATING AGE ON THE HEAD LINE

The beginning of a person's life is determined by studying the Head Line on the thumb side of the palm. Later life is read by considering where the Head Line stops. Mid-life is interpreted in the middle of the palm midway between the beginning of the Head Line and its end somewhere on or near the out side edge of the palm.

ESTIMATING AGE ON THE LOVE LINE

Early life is estimated to start where the Love Line begins on the thumb-side of the hand. The end of this line, usually located near the outside edge of the palm under the Mount of Mercury, represents later years of life.

ESTIMATING AGE ON THE CAREER LINE

The beginning of life is determined at the start of this line near the base of the palm close to the wrist. Wherever this line starts, even if it starts in the middle of the hand, its timeline will be gauged as follows: birth is viewed near the wrist, middle life is approximated to be in the middle of the hand, and later life is measured near the base of the fingers.

LINE VARIATIONS

Unusual marks on the lines can appear in various sizes and shapes. When trying to access the meaning of line variations, first determine what quality the line represents. For example, if you are looking at the Love Line, the subject of romance, emotions, or intimacy will be main topics of discussion.

Next, access the variation on the line that you are viewing. Look at its distinguishing mark(s) and explore what you are looking at on a symbolic level. Be open-minded and free associate possibilities for interpretation(s).

For example, if there is a fork at the beginning of the Love Line and one of the forked lines goes up toward the Mount of Jupiter and the other line trails down toward the Head Line, you need to interpret this branching line in relation to these two locations. You might interpret this forked line to mean that the person's emotional nature is divided between following romantic ideals (one line rising toward Jupiter mount) and over analyzing their emotions (one line branching toward Head Line).

VARIATIONS ON NORMALLY OCCURRING LINE AND INTERPRETATIONS

a/ Extremely long: Extends the range of the line's potential.
b/ Extremely short: Shortens the intensity of the line: no time to waste.
c/ Deep color: Strengthens the depth of interest in this line's subject matter; adds passion.
d/ Wavy lines: Wavering energy, fluctuations, and ambiguities.
e/ Chains (small circles that are connected together within a line): Nervousness—bubbles of tension stressing the nerves.
f/ Islands (singular small circles within a line): Potential problems; health uncertainty, conflict or stress.
g/ Dots: (noticeable bumps or marks within a line that look like a period at the end of a sentence): Illness—stagnant, blocked, or congested energy patterns.
h/ Broken lines: Transitions—breaks in the force of line's energy, or changes in conscious awareness.
i/ Forked lines: Versatility—ideas going in more than one direction, a divided path.
j/ Double lines or sister lines: Increases possibilities and doubles the potential of whatever energy is represented.

REFLECTIONS AND NOTATIONS : CHAPTER SEVEN

Please take time to contemplate and answer the following questions on a separate sheet or enter in your book. Please enter today's date:

Did you notice anything unusual about any major line(s) when you took someone's hand, or looked at your own hand? What did this uncommon quality represent?

What attributes correspond to double lines?

Explain the qualities of a Love Line that has an island.

How do you gauge age or determine time lines when studying your own Love Line, Head Line, and Career Line?

{ CONTINUED }

REFLECTIONS AND NOTATIONS : CHAPTER SEVEN
{ CONTINUED }

Look at your own hand. Determine the point on your Life Line that marks when you were fifteen years old.

What might you tell someone who has a meandering Head Line?

Think about your discussions with people in relation to looking at their palms. What could or should you have said differently or perhaps even more tactfully?

Use the following space to record any memorable comments people made to you, or your most significant reflections concerning your palm reading experiences:

PALMISTRY TIP NO. 8

DON'T BE TOO QUICK TO DEFINE SOMEONE BY CATEGORIZING TRAITS.
YOU CAN LABEL THE LINE, BUT YOU CAN'T LABEL
THE PERSON.

CHAPTER EIGHT

The Minor Lines: So Many Lines, So Little Time

"

IF THERE ARE MANY LINES AND THEY ARE THIN,

WE KNOW THAT THE BRAIN IS OVERACTIVE AND WEAKENED

BY GOING IN TOO MANY DIRECTIONS.

"

EDITH NILES

COMMON MINOR LINES

As you become more experienced reading the major lines in the hand, it will be become apparent that minor lines also play a significant role in determining behavior. Because personality is not defined or decoded by any one line, even minor lines can reveal insights and valuable clues to character analysis.

Before you begin your study of minor lines, it is beneficial to have familiarity with the major lines and their interpretations that were discussed in chapter six. Can you recognize them? If so, it's time to begin your study of the minor lines and their influence.

Think of minor lines as arrows that point to subtle distinctions of behavior. The information you acquire through the study of the network of minor lines will add depth to your discussion. If you do not see any minor lines, don't be alarmed: some hands lack minor lines, other hands will only have one or two, and you'll see some hands which possess most all of the minor lines.

The following listing describes the most significant minor lines and essential keywords for their interpretation. Please refer to the diagram on page 21.

LINE OF MERCURY

This line starts somewhere near the bottom or middle of the palm in or near the Mount of the Moon and continues upward until it ends within the Mount of Mercury. A strong, long, unbroken long line suggests a person who is mentally and physically energetic and in a hurry to find success or to become monetarily wealthy. A broken Line of Mercury indicates that the person may struggle with procrastination or have difficulty with finances. If the line appears short and bright red, it often represents a stressful focus on money concerns.

LINE OF MERCURY KEYWORDS
Inventiveness, focus, business concerns

LINE OF HEPATICA OR LIVER LINE

The Line of Hepatica is sometimes read as the Line of Mercury, but it is a separate line. This line starts near the Mount of the Venus and continues upward to the Mount of Mercury. A lack of this line represents strong vitality, good health, or a life without health concerns. If this line is deep, it indicates that a person will focus on concerns about their health. A line that has a yellow hue indicates liver problems, while a deep red line can be circulation or heart concerns. If other parts of the hand show emotional or mental problems, the presence of this line can represent subconscious addictions.

LINE OF HEPATICA OR LIVER LINE KEYWORDS
Health, personal welfare, capacity for healing

LINE OF THE SUN, OR THE APOLLO LINE OR LINE OF FAME

The beginning of the line is located somewhere under the ring finger (Mount of Apollo) and continues downward. The end of the line is often located somewhere on the Mount of Apollo, but it can also extend farther down the palm in various directions. If the end of the Line of Apollo touches the Love Line, passion will likely infuse the creative traits associated with this line. If the end of the line goes into the Mount of the Moon, intuition will be artistically expressed or there may be a focus on visionary endeavors.

LINE OF THE SUN, APOLLO OR LINE OF FAME KEYWORDS
Creative ability, beauty or intelligence through artistic design,
hunger for fame and fortune

GIRDLE OF VENUS

This crescent shaped line is found between the Love Line and the top of the palm. It extends between the fingers of Apollo and Jupiter. It is the line common in sensitive people who have a hard time hiding their feelings or making decisions about their emotional direction. Most often, people with have this line try to avoid competitive social games.

GIRDLE OF VENUS KEYWORDS
Sensuality, affection, sexuality, sensitivity

MARRIAGE LINE(S)

This horizontal line(s) is found on the outside of the palm under the finger of Mercury above the Love Line. From the outside of the hand these lines can extend a little bit or a long way into the palm. A long singular line represents a strong marriage. A broken or hairline marriage line indicates commitment conflicts. Two or more lines can indicate multiple marriages or deep connections with more than one partner.

MARRIAGE LINE(S) KEYWORDS
Commitment, marriage, loving relationships

CHILDREN LINE(S)

Each line represents one child or commitments of the heart that are similar to an attachment to a child. These short vertical lines run into the horizontal marriage line. Each of these lines represents the potential for one child. (For some people without children, their love for their dog or cat is comparable to the love some people have for a child. In such instances, one of these lines can represent this kind of love.)

CHILDREN LINE(S) KEYWORDS
Children, emotional bonds

RING OF SOLOMON

This curving line looks like a hook, loop, or ring that outlines—or partially circles—the Mount of Jupiter. It suggests a philosophical nature, strong intuition, and the ability to see deeply into people's hearts and minds. Most psychics will have this line as it indicates that their intuitive sense is developed.

RING OF SOLOMON KEYWORDS
Mediums, mysticism, soulfully insightful, spirituality

LINE OF INTUITION

This is a long crescent shaped line within or surrounding the Mount of the Moon. It indicates an intuitive nature as well as the potential for empathy or perception that exists beyond the radar of the conscious mind. The person who has this line is likely to remember their dreams, have a good memory, and reflect on the deeper meaning of important events.

LINE OF INTUITION KEYWORDS
Intuitive abilities, a reflective or empathetic nature

MYSTIC CROSS

This mark looks like a cross or an x that exists within the middle of the Quadrangle on the palm. It can appear large or small, straight up and down, slanted, or sideways as it sits in this horizontal space that exists between the Love Line and Head Line.

MYSTIC CROSS KEYWORDS
Love of metaphysics or philosophy, transpersonal interests, spiritual mindedness

TRAVEL LINES

These horizontal lines within the Mount of the Moon appear close to the bottom of the hand near the outside edge of the palm. Since the person who has this type of line(s) enjoys doing new things, they are often adventurous and are known to make point of going beyond their normal boundaries. If a Travel Line is exceptionally long and touches the Career Line, a person will travel in their work.

TRAVEL LINES KEYWORDS
Love of travel, thinking outside the box

BRACELETS OR RASCETTES

Often you will see three horizontal lines just outside the foundation of the palm where the wrist meets the hand. "No time to lose" is the motto that best describes the person who has three clearly defined lines. Three or more unbroken lines equal a happy, determined nature. While three lines is considered fortunate, less than three lines can indicate that a person has considerable work to do to transform their dreams into reality.

BRACELETS OR RASCETTES KEYWORDS
Quality of life, enjoyment of life

SIGNS AND SYMBOLS

Various marks may appear anywhere on the lines, the mounts, the palm, or even the back of the hand. It's unusual for a hand not to have any signs, or symbols. When you notice a mark, look at its shape, size, and location on the hand and explore its potential symbolic meaning. The following is a list of some of the signs or marks you might find when looking at the palm along with some interpretive keywords:

SIGNS		KEYWORD MEANINGS
▲ }	Triangle	Auspiciousness, good fortune, positive forces
★ }	Star	Illumination, light, shining talent
✝ }	Cross	Bearing heavy responsibility or mystical awareness
# }	Grille	Cross currents of energy, contradicting forces
❑ }	Square	Security issue, home is a central focus

Most importantly, the location of a mark is fundamental to your interpretation. If a mark is on a mount, you should discuss it in relation to the mount's significance. For example, if a triangle sits on the Mount of Venus, your discussion should be in relation to love and romance; it can indicate good luck in love or a lover's triangle. If a symbol or mark sits on a line, it should be discussed in relation to the significance of the line. For instance, if a star sits on the Career Line, you will discuss this mark in relation to the person's career path. It may be considered a mark of opportunity, or the point where a person becomes enlightened about their occupation.

REFLECTIONS AND NOTATIONS : CHAPTER EIGHT

Please take time to contemplate and answer the following questions on a separate sheet or enter in your book. Please enter today's date:

What questions were you most frequently asked when you looked at different hands?

How might you interpret a triangle on the Mount of Jupiter—or the Mount of Saturn—in a person's hand?

What line indicates marriage? What might you say to a person who has two marriage lines, but has only been married once? (Hint: Don't tell a person who is presently married that they will be getting a divorce.)

Where do you locate the Line of the Sun? How would you interpret a short (weak) Line of the Sun? A long (strong) line of the Sun?

What might you tell someone who has three rascettes?

Have you had any negative feedback or responses when doing palm readings? If so, how did you react or overcome this?

Examine your own hand, and answer the palm reading question: "How many children will I have?"

Use the following space to record any memorable comments people made to you, or your most significant reflections concerning your palm reading experiences:

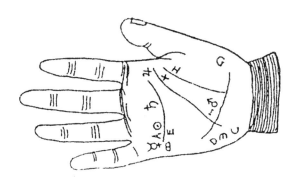

PALMISTRY TIP NO. 9

YOU CANNOT SOLVE OTHER PEOPLE'S PROBLEMS, BUT YOU CAN OFFER INSIGHT THAT CREATES HOPE FOR SUCCESSFUL RESOLUTION.

CHAPTER NINE

Your Passport to Success

BY OVERLOOKING MINUTE SIGNS
YOU WILL MISS A WEALTH OF INFORMATION FOR
THE FORMULATION OF CORRECT JUDGMENT.

JAGAT BRIGHT

DISCUSSING THE MOST POPULAR TOPICS

To be a successful palmist, you must know how to talk about what is most important to people. Although each reading is unique, you will hear certain questions frequently asked by clients. Can you guess what they are?

The most popular questions concern love, money, and health. You should expect many people to ask the following: Does he/she love me? When will I get married or find love? Will I win the lottery? Will I be successful? How is my health? It is important that you know where to look on the palm to answer these and similar questions.

The following listing provides guidance about where and what to look for on the hand so that you can answer the most common questions.

SIGNIFICANT CHARACTERISTICS OF THE MOST POPULAR TOPICS

TO ANSWER QUESTIONS ABOUT LOVE, CONSIDER THE FOLLOWING
1 / Look at the marriage line(s).
2 / How long and deep is the Love Line?
3 / Is the Love Line broken or unbroken?
4 / How high is the Mount of Venus?
5 / Do any lines from inside the Mount of Venus touch or cross the Life Line?

TO ANSWER QUESTIONS ABOUT CAREER SUCCESS, CONSIDER THE FOLLOWING:
1 / How long is the Career Line? Is it broken or forked?
2 / Is the Career Line deep?
3 / How strong is the Mount of Jupiter and/or Mercury?
4 / Is there a star on the Mount of Jupiter?
5 / Where does the Career Line end?

{ CONTINUED }

SIGNIFICANT CHARACTERISTICS OF
THE MOST POPULAR TOPICS

{ CONTINUED }

TO ANSWER QUESTIONS ABOUT WEALTH, CONSIDER THE FOLLOWING:

1 / Is there a large triangle (fortune) covering the center of the palm?
2 / What is the length and shape of the Jupiter finger?
3 / Is the thumb strong and long?
4 / Do you see a strong Mount of Mercury?
5 / Is there a star on the Mount of Jupiter?
6 / Does the Life Line start on the Mount of Jupiter?

TO ANSWER QUESTIONS ABOUT HEALTH, CONSIDER THE FOLLOWING:

1 / Are nails clear and bright colored, or dull and lifeless?
2 / Does the Mount of Saturn have crossed lines or a grille?
3 / Is the Line of Hepatica (health) broken or unbroken?
4 / Does any major line have noticeable dots or islands?
5 / Does the Head Line extend downward and nearly touch the wrist?

TO ANSWER QUESTIONS ABOUT SPIRITUALITY, CONSIDER THE FOLLOWING:

1 / Is there a Line of Intuition?
2 / Do you see a Solomon's Ring on the Mount of Jupiter?
3 / Is there a Mystic Cross in the center of the Quadrangle?
4 / Is there a well-defined Mount of Moon?
5 / Does the Line of Apollo go past the Love Line toward the Mount of Moon?
6 / Do you see any triangles on the Mount of Jupiter?

TO ANSWER QUESTIONS ABOUT HAPPINESS, CONSIDER THE FOLLOWING:

1 / Are the hands and thumb firm yet flexible?
2 / Are there three unbroken Rascettes?
3 / Is there a long line or star on the Mount of Apollo?
4 / Is the Life Line strong and deep?
5 / Is the Love Line deep without frequent small cross lines?
6 / Is the Mount of Venus high and well defined?

A SHORT DEMONSTRATION READING OF THE HAND

What are the most important questions or needs of the person for whom you are doing the reading? Does one topic have more significance and value than other potential focal points? When possible, determine the main focus of your reading. The following demonstration reading was given to a person who asked a question about love:

QUESTION ASKED
I've had trouble staying close to people and developing intimate relationships, especially with a man in my life. Will I have a relationship in my future?

FIRST OBSERVATION: LARGE MOUNT OF MOON
Your Mount of Moon is extremely large and has a cross on it indicating that you may have trouble letting go of the past. Perhaps you have some memories that are creating fear in present time and blocking your emotional trust. You need to be alert to your own mental impressions or emotional anxieties, which may be triggering a negative attitude about relationships. What stops you from staying close to people? If you've had a bad relationship and hold on to the memories of the pain, all of your attention will be focused on your doubts, and you'll be afraid to open your heart.

SECOND OBSERVATION: THE MOUNT OF VENUS IS FLAT
Your flat Mount of Venus shows that you need to build and exercise your emotional courage to talk about your feelings. It takes willpower and confidence to break through old mental patterns that make you step back from reaching for a new relationship. Perhaps you can attend a personal growth workshop that would help you process your feelings and get you more in touch with your flirting nature and your ability to have intimate relationships. It's hard to start a new relationship if you're too shy or focusing on your insecurity. However, this star on your Mount of Venus is significant of your potential to act in loving ways and enhance your emotional perspective. The line crossing from the Mount of Venus toward your Head Line indicates you have courage to look for opportunities to expand your emotional horizon.

THIRD OBSERVATION: A LONG, DEEP LOVE LINE CURVING TOWARD THE MOUNT OF JUPITER
This line's position is significant of the positive outcome or results of your efforts

{ CONTINUED }

A SHORT DEMONSTRATION READING OF THE HAND

{ CONTINUED }

because its depth is linked with the search for love, pleasure, and happiness. It is very favorable because it indicates that even if you've had challenges in past relationships, you should be able to make new friendships and reach for positive opportunities.

FOURTH OBSERVATION: ONE, LONG DEEP MARRIAGE LINE

Also, your strongly defined marriage line indicates that if love is your goal, chances are very good that you'll find it. Be more willing to get in touch with your inner romantic.

A LITTLE PIZZAZZ GOES A LONG WAY

Everyone has their own communication style for giving readings. Each time you give a reading your techniques and skills will evolve, and you will become more familiar with nonverbal as well as vocal play of interpersonal dynamics.

If your words are energizing, your readings will be power packed. For those of you who want guidance as to what suggestions you might offer during a palm reading, I present the following examples:

* Your communications with your boyfriend need to be grounded in clarity in order to figure out what decisions you want to make about your future love life.

* Let your own feelings guide you to the truth of what's inside your heart.

* Take a little time to recharge your energy so you can increase your focus on how to fulfill your goals.

* Instead of always worrying so much about the future, enjoy the now of this moment.

* Have you ever heard the quote: "Love like you've never been in love before?"

REFLECTIONS AND NOTATIONS : CHAPTER NINE

Please take time to contemplate and answer the following questions on a separate sheet or enter in your book. Please enter today's date:

What was most interesting to you when you took someone's hand?

Could you determine what it meant on a symbolic level?

When you look at someone's hand experiment with using your sixth sense to intuit if the person is happy, sad, glad, or mad. To what degree are you using your intuition?

Examine your own hand and lines, and answer this popular palm reading question: "Will I find love in my future?"

Can you be objective when reading your own hand?

{ CONTINUED }

REFLECTIONS AND NOTATIONS : CHAPTER NINE
{ CONTINUED }

What questions were you most frequently asked when you looked at different hands?

What will you look for in a person's hand to answer a question about career possibilities?

Have your tried to read someone's hand when you're tired? How does it feel different than when you feel energetic?

Use the following space to record any memorable comments people made to you, or your most significant reflections concerning your palm reading experiences:

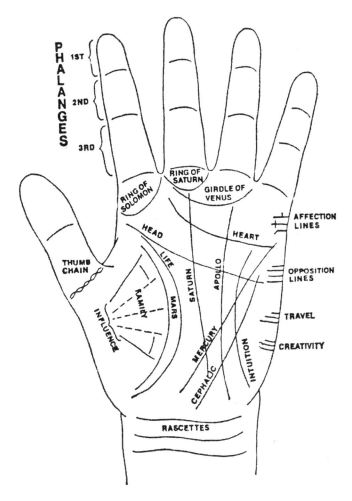

PALMISTRY TIP NO. 10

ALTHOUGH READING SOMEONE'S HAND CAN BRING UP SERIOUS MATTERS, SUCH AS THE LOSS OF A LOVED ONE, BE SURE TO FIND WAYS TO BALANCE THE NEGATIVE WITH THE POSITIVE! AN OPTIMISTIC, UPBEAT APPROACH WILL ENHANCE YOUR READINGS AND HELP YOU SUCCEED.

CHAPTER TEN

The Profit or the Prophet?

> *WORDS SHOULD GIVE LOVE AND WARMTH, NOT HEAT AND SMOKE.*
>
> MATA AMRITANANDAMAYI

EFFORT IS KEY

Hopefully by now you feel confident enough with your studies to practice doing palm readings with your friends, relatives, and acquaintances. Whether at first you perceive this mystical art as straight forward or complicated, if you persevere, chances are you will become good at reading hands. The palm is the mirror to the soul, and the secret to hand analysis is looking deeply into the reflections of character that you can observe from the palm. Adopt a positive attitude and develop confidence. Even if you are sometimes wrong, just keep trying. With persistent effort, as my mentor persuasively told me: "You can do it!"

A PALM READER'S CODE OF ETHICS

Legally, you are not allowed to discuss prescription drugs, give medical advice, or give legal counsel. If you don't feel good about your connection with someone, don't give this person a reading. And:

* Do keep every reading completely confidential.
* Don't make decisions for people.
* Don't be a doom slayer or spew negativity.
* Don't preach self-righteousness.
* Don't make predictions about a pending time of death.
* Don't spend a long time talking about yourself.
* Do encourage positive alternatives to difficult situations.
* Do leave your client feeling hopeful and inspired.

Although some of the above information may seem obvious to you, these guidelines are explicit because they each have either legal or moral consequence. Your professional ethics play a significant role in determining the effect of your interaction with others. If your reading makes your client feel as though they are on a wild roller-coaster

{ CONTINUED }

A PALM READER'S CODE OF ETHICS
{ CONTINUED }

ride, chances are they won't want to come back to you. The outcome of your readings is important, not only for your client, but also for your success. However great your insights, it is your discretion and diplomacy that will make you a valuable palmist.

Also, it's good to know the law in your state that governs fortune telling because historically there have been laws claiming palmistry to be illegal or "the work of the devil". For instance, North Carolina has recently been known to enforce its anti-divination law finding "phrenology, palmistry, clairvoyance, fortune-telling and crafts of a similar kind" a misdemeanor punishable by fines and/or imprisonment unless you are working within a church or a school.

A VALUABLE PRACTICE: MAKING PALM PRINTS

Palm prints can be useful because they allow you to study the hand at your leisure or do palm readings from a distance. However, you do not get to see the top of the hand, feel its texture and temperature, or have the exact definition of finger shapes.

Prints also provide good historical records of past readings that you have done. Once you take a person's palm print, file it away. Later, you can compare it to the lines in the same hands. Since lines commonly change, the palm print will provide a systematic record of the changes that have taken place over time. Also, if you have the technology accessible, scan prints into your computer.

One easy way to do a palm print is to take a photograph of the hand. Easier yet, ask the person to go to a print shop and make a photocopy of their hands. Instruct them to make a photocopy of each hand separately. It is beneficial to ask for at least two prints of each hand from two slightly different angles.

{ CONTINUED }

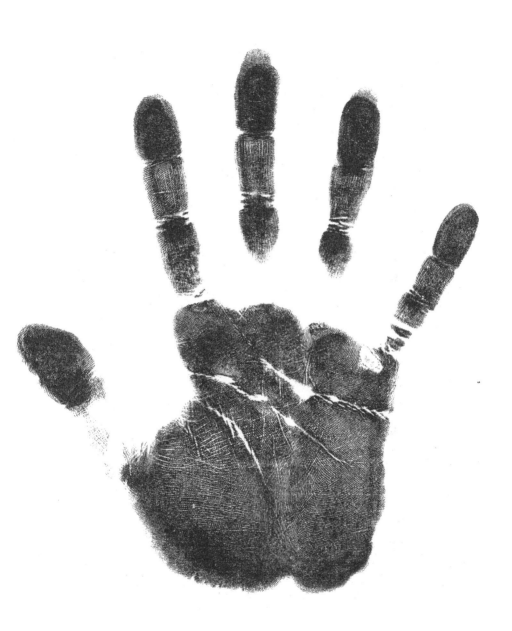

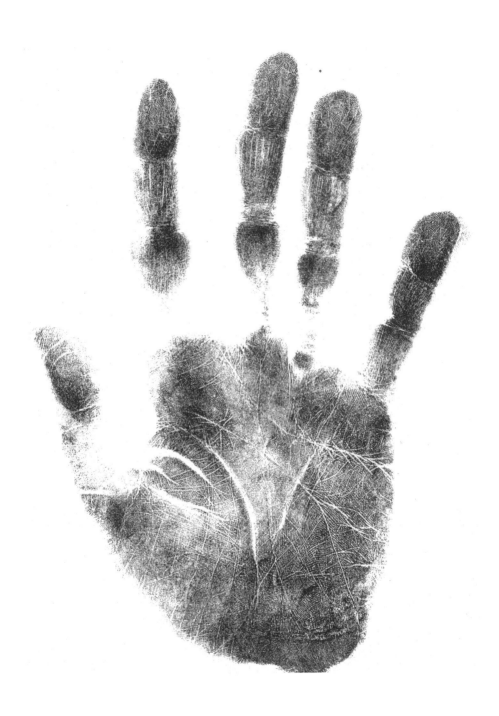

A VALUABLE PRACTICE: MAKING PALM PRINTS
{ CONTINUED }

Before palmists had the option of taking Xerox prints of hands, they took palm prints using paper, a tube of water-based ink, and a rubber roller. The following basic steps will enable you to take a palm print in this manner:

a } First, have quality paper ready to make your print.

b } Take ink out of tube, put on plate, and evenly rub ink on roller.

c } Use evenly inked roller to place ink on a person's palm.

d } Place inked palm firmly on clean paper to make an impression. Do not move the hand once it is on the paper.

e } Check to make sure you have a good print. If not, repeat this above process on clean paper.

f } Let palm print paper dry.

g } Finally, clean hand, plate and roller.

All of the items necessary for making palm prints are available at art supply stores. You can also purchase ready to use finger and palm print taking kits, (used by crime labs). These kits usually feature all all of the necessary equipment and include cleaning cloths.

Whatever method you decide to use for taking palm prints, make sure you use an organized system to file your information. You are guaranteed to make a good impression when you take out someone's palm print that you recorded five years earlier and examine it to make a comparative study.

REFLECTIONS AND NOTATIONS : CHAPTER TEN

Please take time to contemplate and answer the following questions on a separate sheet or enter in your book. Please enter today's date:

What will you say to someone who asks if their hand shows that they will win the lottery?

What will you look for in a person's hand to explain their emotional potential for future happiness?

Are you legally allowed to offer medical advice during a palm reading?

Examine your own hand, and answer the palm reading question: "What career path should I take in the near future?"

How could you interpret a scar or a beauty mark on the Mount of Mercury that looks like a star?

How might you recharge your energy after giving a reading?

Use the following space to record any memorable comments made to you, or your most significant reflections concerning your palm reading experiences:

RECORDING PALM PRINTS

The following information should be recorded on your palm prints. Please record on individual sheets of paper:

ON EACH PAGE RECORD:

Person's Name
Date of Hand Print
Hand Shape
Finger Type
Most Significant Qualities

ADDITIONAL PALMISTRY RESOURCES

Fred Gettings, *The Book of the Hand*
William G. Benham, *The Laws of Scientific Hand Reading*
Cheiro, *Language of the Hand*

NOTES

Introduction: M.M Gaafar, Ilm-Ul-Kaff, *The Science of Hand Reading*, p. 1. And Victor Daniels and Kooch Daniels, *Matrix Meditations*, p. 322.

Chapter One: Fred Gettings, *The Book of the Hand*, p. 27.

Chapter Two: Nathaniel Altman, *Sexual Palmistry*, p. 28.

Chapter Three: Caroline W. Casey, *Making the Gods Work For You*, p. 15.

Chapter Four: William G. Benham, *The Laws of Scientific Hand Reading*, p. 29.

Chapter Five: Cheiro, *Language of the Hand*, p. 72.

Chapter Six: Fred Gettings, *The Book of the Hand*, p. 125.

Chapter: Seven: Ghanshyam Singh Birla, *Destiny in the Palm of Your Hand*, p. 88.

Chapter Eight: Edith Niles, *Complete Hand Reading For the Millions*, p. 107.

Chapter Nine: Jagat Bright, *The Dictionary of Palmistry*, p. 109,

Chapter Ten: Mata Amritanandamayi, edited by Janine Canan, *Messages From Amma*, p. 124.

BIBLIOGRAPHY

Altman, Nathaniel, *Sexual Palmistry*, Wellingborough, Northamptonshire, The Aquarian Press, 1986.

Benham, William, *The Laws of Scientific Hand Reading*, New York, N.Y., Hawthorn Books, 1946.

Birla, Ghanshyam Singh, *Destiny in the Palm of Your Hand*, Rochester, Vermont, Destiny Books, 2000.

Bright, Jagat, *The Dictionary of Palmistry*, New York, N.Y., Bell Publising Co. 1958.

Canan, Janine editor, Mata Amritanandamayi, *Messages From Amma*, Berkeley, Ca. Celestial Arts, 2004.

Casey, Caroline, *Making the Gods Work For You*, New York, N.Y., Harmony Books, 1998.

Cheiro, *Language of the Hand*, first self-published in 1894. Published 1900 by Nicols & Co., Rand, McNally & Co.

Daniels and Daniels, *Matrix Meditations*, Rochester, Vermont, Destiny Books, 2009.

Gettings, Fred, *The Book of the Hand*, Feltham, Middlesex, Hamlyn Publishing Group, 1965.

Niles, Edith, *Complete Hand Reading For the Millions*, Los Angeles, California, Sherbourne Press, 1970.

KOOCH DANIELS — AUTHOR

Early in life Kooch traveled to India to study with a palm reader and this experience was a turning point in becoming a professional hand reader. As well as spending time enjoying her family, she has devoted her life to learning divination and studying Eastern traditions. Seeking balance for her love of metaphysics, she obtained an M.A. in psychology at Sonoma State University.

In addition to her private practice as a professional intuitive, she has worked for twenty-five years as a reader at the Northern and Southern Renaissance Fairs in California where she has given many thousands of palm readings.

With Victor Daniels, she co-authored Matrix Meditations Connecting the Mind and the Heart (Inner Traditions 2009) and Tarot D'Amour (Redwheel Weiser, 2003). She designed the program and created the interpretations for computer generated Tarot Reports for ACS, Astro Computing Services.

For palmistry discussions please visit www.cybermystic.com.

FINAL WORD

*Practice,
practice,
practice
and practice
some more.*

Made in the USA
Middletown, DE
28 February 2015